Archaeology of Aboriginal Culture Change in the Interior Southeast

Ripley P. Bullen Monographs
in Anthropology and History, Number 6
The Florida State Museum

Ripley P. Bullen Monographs in Anthropology and History

Jerald T. Milanich, *editor*

Archaeology of Aboriginal Culture Change in the Interior Southeast

Depopulation during the Early Historic Period

Marvin T. Smith

UNIVERSITY PRESSES OF FLORIDA
UNIVERSITY OF FLORIDA PRESS /
THE FLORIDA STATE MUSEUM
GAINESVILLE

Library of Congress Cataloging in Publication Data

Smith, Marvin T.
  Archaeology of aboriginal culture change in the interior Southeast.

  (Ripley P. Bullen monographs in anthropology and history; no. 6)
  Bibliography: p.
  Includes index.
  1. Indians of North America—Southern States—Social conditions. 2. Indians of North America—Southern States—Population. 3. Indians of North America—Southern States—Antiquities. 4. Diseases and history—Southern States. 5. Southern States—Antiquities. I. Title. II. Series.

E78.S65S56 1987   975'.01   86–32469
ISBN 0–8130–0846–8

UNIVERSITY PRESSES OF FLORIDA is the central agency for scholarly publishing of the State of Florida's university system, producing books selected for publication by the faculty editorial committees of Florida's nine public universities: Florida A&M University (Tallahassee), Florida Atlantic University (Boca Raton), Florida International University (Miami), Florida State University (Tallahassee), University of Central Florida (Orlando), University of Florida (Gainesville), University of North Florida (Jacksonville), University of South Florida (Tampa), University of West Florida (Pensacola).

ORDERS for books published by all member presses should be addressed to University Presses of Florida, 15 NW 15th Street, Gainesville, FL 32603.

To Charlie, who taught me the art of
anthropology,
and to Dave, who taught me the craft of
archaeology

Contents

Contents

Tables

Figures

Acknowledgments

THIS study is the culmination of years of research interest in the early historic period. I have attempted to acknowledge all of the people who have given me considerable assistance, but it is inevitable that someone will be left out by accident. I sincerely apologize to anyone who may have been overlooked.

My interest in the early historic period grew out of fieldwork with David Hally at the Little Egypt site (1970–72) and with Patrick Garrow and Hally at the King site (1973–74). I owe both of these gentlemen a great debt. Their support and friendship throughout the years have been greatly appreciated.

This study would not have been possible without the availability of data from private collections. I am particularly indebted to Richard and Juanita Battles, Jon Peek, and Steve Hunter for allowing me to study their collections.

Numerous individuals also allowed access to unpublished data. Frank Schnell supplied data from the Abercrombie site, Mary Elizabeth Good furnished information on the Tallassee site in Alabama, Paul Parmalee allowed access to the McClung Museum notes and collections from several sites in Tennessee, Mark Williams furnished valuable discussions of the Scull Shoals and Joe Bell sites, Keith Little furnished information about the King site sword, Caleb Curren supplied additional Alabama data, and Vernon J. Knight, Jr., supplied comments and criticisms and made available data from the University of Alabama site files. James B. Langford provided much information about the Coosawattee Valley.

The contributions of Richard Polhemus must be singled out. He freely shared his detailed knowledge of eastern Tennessee with me both in discussions and in a manuscript that he has been preparing for publication. Although Richard's name appears throughout the text, the citations do not cover the scope of his assistance. The hospitality shown me by Richard and his parents during a data-collecting expedition to Knoxville will long be remembered.

I also owe a great debt to Charles Hudson of the University of Georgia and to Chester DePratter of the University of South Carolina. After years of collaboration in researching the explorations of Hernando de Soto and Juan Pardo, it is often difficult to separate our thoughts on the early historic period. Much that appears here can no doubt be attributed to them.

Wallace Reservoir data were generously supplied by David Hally, Mark Williams, Gary Shapiro, Jerald Ledbetter, Dan Elliot, and James Rudolph. Rudolph in particular must be thanked for providing the results of his rim sherd analysis.

Ann Ramenofsky provided a copy of her excellent dissertation late in my project. This allowed me to avoid duplicating much of her research on specific diseases. Many of our methods were quite similar but independently derived. I hope that she will find this study as interesting as I found hers.

L. B. Jones and Carrie Avent have assisted me to a great extent in my quest for knowledge about glass trade beads. Their contribution to this research cannot be overlooked.

Charles Fairbanks, Jerald Milanich, Kathleen Deagan, Theron Nunez, and Michael Gannon served as my doctoral dissertation committee at the University of Florida. Their knowledge of southeastern archaeology, history, and ethnohistory made their contributions numerous. This work, revised from that dissertation, nonetheless reflects much input from the original committee. Their suggestions, organizational skills, and editorial ability are still reflected in this version.

Charles Fairbanks provided constant encouragement. His fieldwork from Tennessee, Georgia, and Alabama had a direct bearing on this research. Fairbanks worked with the early historic sites of Rymer, Ledford Island, Hiwassee Island, 1Ce101, Tallassee, Abercrombie, and Lamar. In addition to his widespread fieldwork, his pioneering publications on Spanish colonial artifacts made him uniquely suited to supervise this research. He also provided funds for a data-collecting trip to Georgia and Tennessee during the summer of 1983.

In addition to my formal doctoral committee, Jeffrey Brain, Charles Hudson, David Hally, Steve Kowalewski, Gary Shapiro, Robert Wilson, and Ian Brown read early drafts of this work and made many useful comments. The scholarly and emotional support of these friends over the years is greatly appreciated. I also want to thank my parents and grandmother for their years of support. Only through their generosity was I able to pursue my scholarly training.

Patrick and Barbara Garrow, of Garrow & Associates, Inc., allowed me time away from my usual duties to revise the manuscript for publication. I cannot imagine two more generous, supportive employers.

Photographs for this volume were obtained from several sources. Figures 3.3, 3.4, 3.6, 3.7, 3.10c, 4.1, 4.2, 5.1, 5.2, 5.3, 5.4, 5.5, and 5.6 were furnished by Gordon Lee Hight. The King site photographs are used by permission of David J. Hally. Juanita Battles furnished figure 3.5. The author furnished figures 3.2, 3.8, and 3.9. Figure 3.10a was taken by Richard T. Bryant. Figure 3.10b was furnished by Ian Brown and is reproduced with his permission. Figure 7.2 was taken by Maurice Williams. Maps and figures were initially drawn by the author and Robin Teas. David Palmer and Lawrence Leshan prepared all of the figures for publication, and Donna Ruhl helped with the editorial preparation of the manuscript. To each of these persons I offer my sincerest thanks.

1

Problems of Culture Change

THIS study focuses on the various types of culture changes that occurred in the aboriginal chiefdoms of a portion of the interior southeastern United States as a result of European contact. As contact spread throughout the New World, some coastal groups were conquered and used for agricultural labor and others were forced into mission systems (Geiger 1937; Service 1954; Hemming 1978). The aboriginal groups inhabiting the interior southeastern United States largely avoided sustained, direct contact but underwent drastic culture change nevertheless.

There are no direct historical accounts of these changes in the interior populations because no Europeans were present to record them. Understanding the processes of cultural disintegration thus becomes an archaeological problem, and it is this historically undocumented change that is investigated here. The central thesis to be demonstrated is that population collapse, caused by European epidemic diseases, was the major change during the early historic period in interior areas. It will be argued that, outside of areas of prolonged European-Indian contact, for example, the interior Southeast, acculturation had virtually no influence.

The term *interior Southeast* is used to indicate the portion of the southeastern United States north or west of the fall line region and east of the Mississippi Valley. The coastal plain and Florida are thus excluded from consideration. In coastal areas, contact between Europeans and Indians was more intensive and continuous; different patterns of culture change (acculturation) may have taken place there because of the presence of European settlements at such places as St.

1

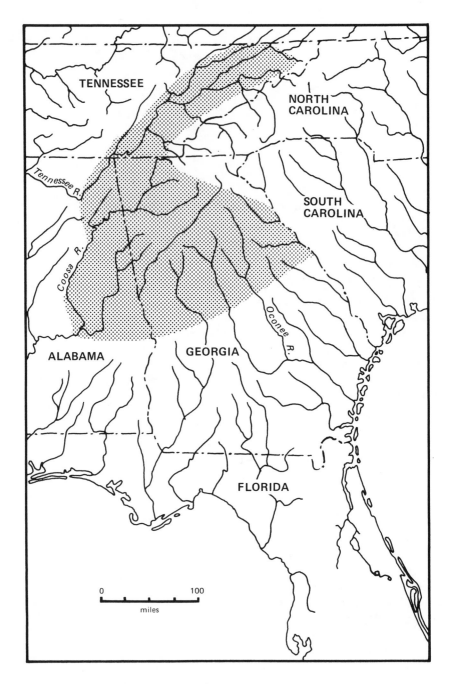

Figure 1.1. Location of the study area.

Augustine and Santa Elena and the Spanish missions along the Atlantic coasts of Florida, Georgia, South Carolina, and Virginia and across northern interior Florida. Acculturation in these settings was quite different from the indirect influences of disease investigated here.

The *study area* examined here is a portion of the interior Southeast (fig. 1.1). It consists of the Georgia and Alabama piedmont and the Ridge and Valley province of Tennessee, Georgia, and Alabama. It is bordered by the upper Alabama River on the west, the fall line to the Savannah River on the east, and the present Bristol, Tennessee, area to the north. The mountainous regions of northern Georgia, eastern Tennessee, and western North Carolina are excluded. The study consists of the drainage areas of the Tennessee River, the Coosa River, the Chattahoochee River, the upper Ocmulgee River, and the upper Oconee River.

Rather than concentrate on a single site or a single locality (e.g., a reservoir), I felt that a broad region was more appropriate for the hypotheses to be investigated. While a few individual sites containing evidence of early European exploration have been described, no one has tried to synthesize the effects of early European exploration within a relatively large area of the Southeast, at least not in archaeological terms. Historians and ethnohistorians have utilized the documentary record to interpret what took place in the interior, but these sources have had little to say about the interior Southeast. Only by combining the meager historical documentation with the archaeological evidence can we hope to gain a reasonably full understanding of the processes that reshaped the southeastern societies.

The *early historic period* is the era when the Spaniards were the only European presence in the study area. It began in 1540 with the expedition of Hernando de Soto and ended with the arrival of English traders from Virginia and South Carolina in the 1670s. Because this is a study of both direct and indirect European influence, it would be appropriate to begin the study somewhat earlier; European goods and diseases filtered into the interior in advance of Europeans (B. Smith 1968:63, 64; Ramenofsky 1982).

Chiefdoms is the term used throughout this study to refer to a specific level of social complexity. They were "ranked societies" in which there was "pervasive inequality of persons and groups" (Service 1962:154). People were socially ranked according to their genealogical nearness to the chief (Service 1962:155). Chiefdoms generally had highly productive economies and centers "which coordinate economic, social, and religious activities" (Service 1962:144). It is clear that the interior Southeast Indian communities at the beginning of the early historic period were organized as chiefdoms.

Demography and early historic period culture change

The demographic collapse of the New World has been the focus of a number of recent studies. Henry Dobyns (1966, 1983), William Denevan (1976), Sherburne Cook and Woodrow Borah (1960), Alfred Crosby (1972), and Ann Ramenofsky (1982) have demonstrated that a cataclysmic decline in population took place following the introduction of the Old World pathogens after 1492. Because we are just now coming to a full realization of the tremendous magnitude of this decline, there has been little attention given to the effects on New World chiefdoms.

For example, in his study of sixteenth-century culture change in Paraguay, Elman Service (1954) does not consider depopulation to be a causal factor. Julian Steward and Louis Faron (1959:176) use the term "deculturation" to designate a type of culture change in which important cultural features are lost. Their best example of deculturation is the Cuña Indians of present Panama.

> It became clear that the Cuña Indians, who are the modern descendants of the Indians buried at Cocle, had been so broken by the Spanish Conquest that their native chiefdoms were destroyed, their social classes eliminated, and their skills in producing art goods in textiles, ceramics, and metallurgy were lost. What remained was primitive society much like that of the Amazonian Indians. That is, the Cuña retained the simple features of their native village life, but lost the institutions and skills associated with chiefdoms and social classes. (Steward and Faron 1959:176)

Although Steward and Faron have introduced a useful concept in "deculturation," they do not describe the process; rather, they contrast the Cuña as described in sixteenth-century accounts left by Spanish explorers and archaeologically recovered evidence of prehistoric Cuña life-style with modern Cuña culture, demonstrating that virtually all "higher" levels of political, religious, and craft aspects of culture have been lost. Furthermore, they do not tie the process they call deculturation to population loss. Indeed, in speaking of the chiefdoms of northern Venezuela, they point out that early Spanish conquest led to the area's depopulation: "The surviving Indians retreated into the forests, where they were soon deculturated to an unstratified, simple village or folk level of society" (Steward and Faron 1959:241). That is, they seem to view deculturation as a later process than depopulation and dispersement, not a concurrent aspect of one phenomenon of change.

In what is basically a historical work, John Hemming (1978) has described the collapse of Brazil's native population. While recognizing the importance of the introduction of European diseases, he also stresses the effects of the slave trade and the mission system. He carefully documents the evidence for large Amazonian aboriginal groups described by sixteenth-century explorers and contrasts it with later accounts of abandoned areas; but he does not analyze the process of population decline. What happened in the Amazon basin appears to be similar to what happened in many areas of the New World: It was quickly explored during the sixteenth century; when no valuable commodities were discovered, it was forgotten, then revisited generations later. In that interval, vast changes in the aboriginal population took place. The interior southeastern United States underwent a similar chain of experiences.

Perhaps the only person to consider seriously the specific effects of depopulation on aboriginal cultural organization is Henry Dobyns. In *Their Number Become Thinned* (1983), he suggests that depopulation was severe and that it caused great cultural changes. He discusses settlement amalgamation—the banding together of survivors, settlement shifts to new locations, simplification of social systems, despecialization of economic structure, loss of skilled specialists, and new types of warfare, all resulting from depopulation brought about by epidemics of European disease. We have from Dobyns a model for the changes brought about by disease.

Dobyns uses mostly secondary, translated, historiographic data to demonstrate his thesis that depopulation caused cultural change. His main case study is the Timucuan Indians of Florida, a group that experienced almost constant direct European contact beginning in the 1560s, first with the French (Bennett 1975) and later the Spaniards (Geiger 1937; Lyon 1976; Milanich and Proctor 1978). In these circumstances we cannot be certain that much of the change that Dobyns documents did not result from forces of acculturation. He suggests that similar changes took place in the interior (1983:324) but does not demonstrate it. He does look at some archaeological data from the Seneca of western New York; but because of their importance in the fur trade, the Seneca were in direct contact with Europeans through-out most of the seventeenth century so the changes they underwent might not be due to depopulation alone. Furthermore, Seneca society was not organized at a chiefdom level, and it is the effect of depopula-tion on chiefdoms that is the focus of this study.

Dobyns (1983) has argued that far-reaching pandemics spread in-land from initial coastal contact. Ann Ramenofsky (1982) also has ar-gued that population collapse of interior groups preceded direct con-tact. They may be right. Almost certainly early European explorers penetrating the interior portions of the New World from Canada (Fenton 1940:175) to Brazil (Hemming 1978) also infected the aborigi-nal inhabitants with new diseases. For our purpose here, we accept the view that severe depopulation followed European contact and that even interior areas were affected. Evidence to demonstrate this col-lapse and to document its timing will be assembled, but the main goal is to demonstrate the effects of this depopulation on aboriginal cul-ture, specifically, the collapse of the interior southeastern Indian chiefdoms.

A model of change for the early historic period can be constructed. As population declined through time, we would expect that sites would decline in number and would become smaller. We would ex-pect to find tangible evidence of disease in burial populations, and several measures of disease are presented in chapter 4. Since there is historical evidence that populations moved following epidemics, we would expect to find archaeological evidence of migrations.

The collapse of the aboriginal population brought about changes in sociopolitical organization. The complex chiefdoms described by sixteenth-century explorers (Rangel and Elvas in Bourne 1922; Ban-dera 1569) gave way to eighteenth-century tribal units of refugees de-scribed by later Europeans (discussed in Swanton 1922, 1928, 1946) but the rate of this change is unknown. We hypothesize that it was rapid, following closely upon the population collapse and, indeed, caused by it. It will be argued in chapter 6 that since there was no pro-longed direct European contact, these changes were not the result of acculturation but rather of depopulation.

Goals of the study

Why has the decline of chiefdoms brought about by European contact been so little studied?

Archaeological sites in the Southeast that produced early European artifacts were often mistakenly given eighteenth-century dates; indeed, there is still this tendency on the part of some. Only recently have the artifacts typical of the early historic period been recognized. This research should help to fill a void in the literature and provide a chronological ordering of over fifty archaeological sites, excavated during the past century, as a base from which to look at the cultural changes that took place during the early historic period. The measurement and assessment of these changes caused by depopulation form the basis of this work.

This research will also enhance our knowledge of culture contact, especially the critical timing of cultural and population collapse brought about by European and African contact with the New World. We expect the results to demonstrate that collapse was rapid, probably occurring in less than sixty years. This idea of rapid breakdown has applicability throughout the New World.

The study also concentrates on a specific type of contact situation. In the study area, direct European short-term contact (exploration) was followed by over a century of indirect European influence, primarily the spread of disease. Historical and archaeological data show that drastic culture change took place, yet it is argued that this change was not acculturation. Certainly the processes of change were not the same as those in colonized or missionized areas where a direct European presence was maintained. There are other analogous situations throughout the New World, Amazonia a prime example. This type of culture change has not been studied in detail. What are the indirect effects of a relatively distant European presence?

Most important, we will explore the application of archaeological methods to demonstrate the decline of chiefdoms associated with general population decline. The direct historic approach (Steward 1942) is shown to be invalid for the interior Southeast (and hence for many areas of the New World), the concept of an "indirect historical approach" is introduced and used here. It can be applied to areas where infrequent contact by literate Europeans combined with severe population decline to obscure the history of Native Americans. The indirect historical approach is to work from the historically known to the more recent historically unknown to the even more recent historically known. It has been argued that it is almost impossible to use a direct historical approach to work backward from the well-documented eighteenth-century tribal societies of the study area to their prehistoric chiefdom forebears (Smith 1976:45, Dobyns 1983:338, 342). The only useful approach is to look at the southeastern Indians at the dawn of contact through the eyes of the early Spanish explorers of the six-teenth century. Once an understanding of that period is reached, it can be used as a baseline to work both backward into prehistory and forward to link up with the documented societies of the eighteenth century.

Finally, two different techniques for establishing chronological controls are compared. A seriation of sites based on European trade goods is used in the western portion of the study area, and a seriation based on aboriginal ceramics is used in the eastern portion.

The data base and methodology

Because this research is a synthesis of earlier research, using old data to answer new questions, it must be pointed out that the sites selected were not chosen for excavation specifically to test this work's hypoth-eses. Rather, they include all those thus far located in the study area that have produced European trade objects typical of the early his-toric period (chap. 3). Over fifty sites are represented in various stages of completeness of data. Not all desired variables were collected by all researchers at these sites. Thus, some hypotheses can be tested by a wide range of data from many sites, others with limited data from a few sites. Such are the problems of using data collected by earlier re-searchers for other purposes.

The archaeological data utilized here were collected over a cen-tury, from the late nineteenth century to the 1980s. Data from nine-teenth-century observers for the Smithsonian Institution and the Bu-reau of American Ethnology, other individuals, such as Clarence B. Moore and Warren K. Moorehead, numerous W.P.A. (Work Projects Administration) projects, postwar reservoir salvage projects, and mod-ern contract archaeology are combined with data collected by avoca-tional archaeologists to present the fullest possible picture of culture processes during the early historic period in the study area. This cer-tainly is not a "sample" in the statistical sense, although it is the known complete population of excavated sites (recognizing that the exca-vated sites are not a sample of the total sites). Yet the areas relied upon for the bulk of the interpretations—the Tennessee River drainage and the Coosa River drainage—are among the most thoroughly in-vestigated areas of the Southeast. It can be argued that random re-search, as well as W.P.A. and later surveys in these areas, probably lo-cated most of the large early historic period town and village sites. During the early historic period, small hamlets were not characteristic of the Tennessee Valley (Richard Polhemus, personal communication) or, apparently, of the Coosa drainage; most people in these areas apparently lived in towns. While the sample cannot be justified statistically, it is large and varied enough for the level of interpretation offered here.

Data collected in the Wallace Reservoir Salvage Project of the University of Georgia serve as a check against the Tennessee-Coosa data. The Wallace Reservoir survey is one of the most thorough systematic surveys carried out in the interior Southeast. Over fifteen hundred archaeological sites were located by surface and subsurface techniques during the late 1970s. The survey is a scientific sample; if these data prove to support the same hypotheses confirmed by the "grab sample" from other areas, then we are on firm footing for interpretation of the cultural processes of the early historic period.

When discussing the decrease in the number of sites over time as a possible result of epidemics of European diseases, a large region must be examined so we can take migration into account (Ramenofsky 1982). There is historical documentation of people fleeing diseased areas (see ch. 4). Clearly, in a small area, the number of sites may decline drastically when people move away. By looking at large regions such as river drainage basins or the whole study area, we minimize the effect of migration.

Another methodological safeguard may be found in the different types of chronological controls utilized. In the western drainages of the study area, only sites that have produced datable European artifacts were analyzed. This restriction produced the chronological control necessary to measure culture change in several archaeologically distinctive areas. These areas do not have the fine-scale ceramic chronologies that would provide the control necessary to include sites that may be of the early historic period but that have not yet produced European artifacts. Sites that have not produced a single European artifact could nonetheless have been occupied during the early historic period. Certainly European goods were not present at all sites in the sixteenth century, and the kind of limited archaeological research that has been carried out at most sites is not always adequate to locate any European artifacts that might be there. Indeed, it is remarkable that we have as much tangible evidence of the early European presence, direct and indirect, in the interior Southeast as we do. Nonetheless, circumstances require that only the sites that have produced European goods be used, since other sites lack the necessary chronological control.

Here again the Wallace Reservoir data are important as a check. While sites that produced European artifacts were scarce in the reservoir, stratigraphic excavation and seriation techniques have allowed the construction of a fairly tight chronological sequence of aboriginal ceramics, which provides us with a chronological control. It is possible to differentiate sixteenth-century from seventeenth-century sites with great confidence. The Wallace Reservoir data are drawn from all sites, from mound center to specialized extractive sites (Shapiro 1983), and provide a check for the data based on sites having European artifacts from the other drainages. This point is important. If both sets of data indicate similar processes, then we can be more confident of the interpretations advanced.

2

The Historical Background

THE historic period in the interior Southeast began with explorations by Hernando de Soto in 1540. There are four eyewitness accounts of his expedition: Ranjel (Bourne 1922), Biedma (Smith 1968), A Gentleman of Elvas (Smith 1968), and the recently located Cañete account. Ranjel, de Soto's secretary, gives the most exacting account, and the Elvas account contains much detail. Biedma was the king's factor on the expedition; his short account, which was his official report to the king, provides interesting information. A synopsis of the Cañete account, recently discovered by Eugene Lyon, contains additional information about the Indians of the Southeast. There is also the detailed history of the expedition by Garcilaso de la Vega written some fifty years later (Varner and Varner 1951) based upon his interviews with participants in the expedition. Though overembellished, his account provides much detail on the Southeast of the sixteenth century.

The de Soto expedition was important. De Soto saw a Southeast never again seen (Hudson 1980). He saw many different southeastern cultures, and he saw southeastern chiefdoms while they were fully functional. The Southeast is a diverse region, and de Soto observed and recorded much of it as he trekked from Florida to Texas.

De Soto's primary goal was to obtain wealth in the form of precious metals. He searched near and far and high and low (literally as he entered both the Appalachian and Ozark mountains). He hoped to find a second Mexico or Peru, but his efforts failed and he died on the Mississippi River.

The expedition of Tristan de Luna entered the study area with a different motive. He came to the Southeast in 1559 to colonize, bringing families of Mexican farmers instead of a massive military force.

Luna was to set up colonies on the Gulf and Atlantic coasts and establish communications overland between these areas (Priestley 1928). Although well prepared to meet these goals, the Luna expedition was foiled by a storm, which wrecked several vessels before they could be unloaded. With most of their food supplies lost, the colonists faced starvation. Most of the force moved inland to the Indian town of Nanipacana, whose exact location is unknown. When food grew short there, another group headed north to Coosa. Luna's force included several veterans of the de Soto expedition, and they remembered Coosa as a fertile place (Hudson et al. 1985). At Coosa, they were disappointed in the small villages they found. Coosa was not the bustling capital they remembered. In return for food, the people of Coosa asked the Spaniards to help them in a dispute with their neighbors the Napochies, who refused to pay tribute. A large force of Coosa warriors and Spanish allies set out to the Napochie towns, which they quickly brought under control, and the flow of tribute to Coosa was restored. The Spaniards later left Coosa to return south to their main force. They found Luna's command falling apart, and by 1561 the entire colony had to be rescued and returned to New Spain.

The Luna attempt gives us a glimpse of the interior in the aftermath of the de Soto expedition. In the intervening twenty years, Coosa had lost some of its size and glory and was having trouble collecting tribute from one of its nearest neighbors. Coosa in 1560 appeared to be still in its 1540 location (Hudson et al. 1985). It had no doubt lost population to European disease, but apparently the population had stabilized in the period between the visits of de Soto and Luna. The Luna accounts do give some idea of the location of named groups in 1560.

The last major expedition into the study area during the sixteenth century was led by Captain Juan Pardo. He actually made two trips into the interior between 1566 and 1568 (Hudson et al. 1985), setting out from the newly founded settlement of Santa Elena, on the present Parris Island, South Carolina (South 1980). The Pardo expeditions had multiple motives. There was a shortage of food in the new colony, and Pardo's men were sent to live off the land. And Pardo was sent to discover an overland route to Zacatecas, Mexico.

Unlike the earlier expeditions, Pardo's had no horses. While it was a purely military force, it had specific orders not to upset the Indian populations. Indeed, Pardo was given large quantities of trade goods to distribute to the Indians to secure political alliances and food for his troops (DePratter and Smith 1980).

Marching into the interior of South Carolina, Pardo came upon the same route taken by Hernando de Soto approximately thirty years earlier. He appears to have gone to the the same towns in the same locations visited by de Soto (DePratter et al. 1983). His force marched through present South Carolina, North Carolina, and Tennessee, and some of it apparently reached Coosa in northwestern Georgia. Pardo had a scribe, Juan de la Bandera, who recorded excellent information on the location of Indian groups. Because of the Pardo expedition we are able to reconstruct much of the route of de Soto and to locate aboriginal groups. The Bandera document has become a key to unlocking the sixteenth-century Southeast.

Using information from these exploration accounts, we can reconstruct the distribution of southeastern chiefdoms in the mid-sixteenth century. Using an ethnohistoric-archaeological approach (Brain et al. 1974) to combine data from the accounts with archaeological data such as settlement distribution and the distribution of European trade items, we can locate sixteenth-century chiefdoms with some degree of accuracy.

What was the sixteenth-century Southeast? Charles Hudson (1980) has characterized it as an "unknown South"—a time of flourishing complex chiefdoms, large towns, dense populations, high levels of military organization, complex religion, and elites marked by sumptuary rules. The Southeast described by the early Spanish explorers was a far cry from that described by explorers of the late seventeenth and eighteenth centuries. By that time, the large populations had been reduced by disease and the chiefdoms had been reduced to less complex units, some of which were beginning to form confederacies. Patterns of warfare were changing as firearms were introduced and the English demand for slaves increased (Perdue 1979; Wright 1981). The problem is to identify the processes that transformed the Southeast of the sixteenth century to that of the eighteenth.

The first step is to understand the political organization of the Southeast at the time of initial contact. The study area was made up of several complex chiefdoms and perhaps a few simpler ones. Complex chiefdoms have two or three tiers of political hierarchy (Steponaitis 1978). A good example of such a polity in the study area known from archaeology is the "Great Oconee Province" described by Smith and Kowalewski (1980). The Oconee Province settlement hierarchy consists of a capital with five mounds (Shoulderbone mound group); two multiple mound sites (Shinholser and Scull Shoals); at least two single mound centers (Dyar and 9Ge35); and countless villages, hamlets,

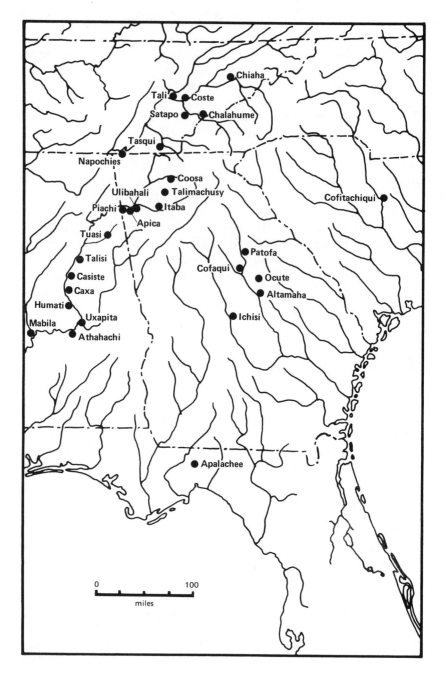

Figure 2.1. Location of sixteenth-century towns.

and special purpose sites (see Rudolph and Blanton 1980; Shapiro 1983). The settlement density of this "province" is impressive, and there seems to be a large, unoccupied buffer zone surrounding the province. Recent work on the route of Hernando de Soto (Hudson et al. 1984) has identified this province as the Ocute mentioned in the de Soto narratives. Thus the Shoulderbone site is the principal town of Ocute, Scull Shoals may be the town of Patofa, and Shinholser appears to be the Altamaha of the narratives.

Analyses of the routes of Hernando de Soto, Tristan de Luna, and Juan Pardo have allowed us to locate many of the towns mentioned in the exploration narratives. By combining descriptions, travel times, and distances given in the narratives with archaeological evidence of contemporary Indian sites (based on ceramic seriations and/or presence of diagnostic European material), we have been able to locate many sixteenth-century Indian polities (Hudson et al. 1984, 1985; DePratter et al. 1983, 1985). These locations are shown in figure 2.1. Named towns of the narratives that can confidently be associated with archaeological sites are listed in table 2.1. These identifications provide the baseline for looking at population decline and movement in the century following and at political restructuring. For example, the narratives frequently identify the political alliances of the various towns, and there is evidence of multiple levels of political organization among the various towns in the chiefdoms. A small village may be said to be under a larger village, which is in turn under yet another principal town of a chiefdom. These political relationships are tabulated in table 2.2.

As stated, the study area was virtually *terra incognita* from 1568 to 1673. Only one expedition seems actually to have entered the area during that interval, while two others visited the interior on the margins of the area. These expeditions are poorly known but require discussion.

In 1596, a soldier named Gaspar de Salas and two Franciscan fathers, Pedro Fernandez de Chosas and Francisco de Veras, left Guale (St. Catherines Island) for the interior (Swanton 1922:176, 181–82). In testimony given four years later, Salas reported on the expedition. Leaving St. Catherines Island, the three reached Tama by traveling eight days, the first seven of which were through deserted land. Tama was no doubt the Altamaha of the de Soto relations (Swanton 1946: 208). Salas leaves no doubt that they had reached the Piedmont: "there is very good brown soil, which, when it rains, clings to one's feet

Table 2.1. Correlations of towns mentioned in sixteenth-century narratives with archaeological sites in the study area, based on research by Charles Hudson, Chester DePratter, and Marvin Smith

PROVINCE Towns within province	Archaeological site	Source
(Independent town)		
Ichisi	Lamar[a]	De Soto narratives
OCUTE		
Altamaha	Shinholser[a]	De Soto
Ocute	Shoulderbone[a]	De Soto
Cofaqui	Dyar[a]	De Soto
Patofa	Scull Shoals	De Soto
(Questionable province affiliations or statuses)		
Chiaha	Zimmerman's Island[a]	De Soto, Pardo
Chiscas	Plum Grove area	De Soto
Coste	Bussell Island	De Soto
COOSA		
Tali	Henry[a]	De Soto
Coosa	Little Egypt	De Soto, Luna
Napochies	Audubon Acres and Citico	Luna
Itaba	Etowah	De Soto
Ulibahali	Coosa Country Club[a]	De Soto, Luna
Village subject to Ulibahali	King or Johnstone	De Soto
Apica	Johnstone	Luna
Piachi	King	De Soto
Tuasi	1Ce308	De Soto
Abandoned town	1Tal72?	De Soto
Talisi	One of Kymulga sites	De Soto
TASCALUÇA		
Uxapita	Taskigi	De Soto
Athahachi	Charlotte Thompson	De Soto
Piachi	Durant's Bend?[a]	De Soto
(Questionable province affiliations or statuses)		
Chalahume	Chilhowee	Pardo
Satapo	Citico 40Mr7	Pardo

a. Sites without early historic period European trade goods (most are unexcavated).

like marl. There are in certain regions many barren hills where he saw many kinds of minerals" (Swanton 1922:182). This is clearly a description of Georgia red clay and piedmont mineral resources. The straight-line distance from St. Catherines Island to the presumed site of Altamaha of the de Soto period, the Shinholser Mound site near Milledgeville, Georgia, is 155 miles. It is certainly possible that three men traveling lightly could make the necessary twenty miles per day. From Tama, the party continued inland one day to Ocute (it took the de Soto expedition one day and part of a second, but they traveled about fifteen miles per day (DePratter et al. 1985). Thus it is likely that Ocute was still in the same general area as de Soto found it, perhaps still at the Shoulderbone site. The cacique of Ocute convinced them that it would be dangerous to continue, and the party returned via a different route to the coast.

Later, in 1606, the chief of Tama traveled to Sapelo Island to meet with Governor Ibarra (Swanton 1922:182). Thus there were at least two documented occasions when European presents were probably given to the Indians of the Province of Ocute around the turn of the century. Indeed, European artifacts of this period have been found at two archaeological sites in the area, site 9Ge948 (Smith 1979a) and the Joe Bell site (Williams 1983). Both sites produced glass beads, and the Joe Bell site also produced peach pits.

In 1628, Pedro de Torres visited Cofitachiqui (Swanton 1922:220), believed to be located near the present Camden, South Carolina (DePratter et al. 1983). Almost nothing is known of this expedition. Torres noted that the area was rich in pearls and that all the chiefs in the area were politically aligned under the chief of Cofitachiqui. While Cofitachiqui is east of the study area, it is in the interior on the fall line; it shows the extent of Spanish influence in the interior, which will be discussed further when early English penetration of the interior is considered.

One final Spanish expedition into the interior of the Southeast west of the study area was the 1634 expedition of Captain Alonzo Baca (Thomas 1982:22–34). Baca set out from Santa Fe, New Mexico, and headed east with some soldiers, eventually reaching the "Great River," which Thomas identifies as the Mississippi. They did not cross it but returned to New Mexico. The directions given in the Baca account are vague, and the identification of the "Great River" with the Mississippi cannot be considered proven; the possibility nevertheless remains that this expedition had some effect on the Southeast.

Table 2.2. Sixteenth-century political relationships according to the de Soto, Luna, and Pardo narratives

Province, chiefdom, or head town	Known or probable subject towns or provinces	Known or probable subject villages
Ichisi (R)		Two villages (R)
Ocute (R)	Altamaha (R)[a] ?Cofaqui (E, R)[b] ?Tatofa (R)[b]	
Patofa (E), a province at peace with Ocute		
Chisca (E, P, R)		
Chiaha (B, R)	Olamico (head town; P)[c]	
	Coste (R)[d] Tali (R)	

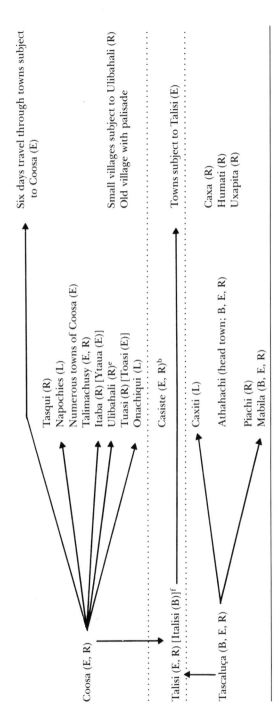

Six days travel through towns subject to Coosa (E)

Tasqui (R)
Napochies (L)
Numerous towns of Coosa (E)
Talimachusy (E, R)
Itaba (R) [Ytaua (E)]
Ulibahali (R)[e]
Tuasi (R) [Toasi (E)]
Onachiqui (L)

Small villages subject to Ulibahali (R)
Old village with palisade

Coosa (E, R)

Casiste (E, R)[b]

Talisi (E, R) [Italisi (B)][f]

Towns subject to Talisi (E)

Caxiti (L)

Athahachi (head town; B, E, R)

Tascaluça (B, E, R)

Piachi (R)
Mabila (B, E, R)

Caxa (R)
Humati (R)
Uxapita (R)

SOURCES: B = Biedma; E = Elvas; G = Garcilaso; L = Luna; P = Pardo; R = Ranjel.

NOTE: Arrows denote political relationships documented in narratives (e.g., tribute paid); other relationships are probable. Alternative spellings are in brackets.

a. Biedma says Altamaha is a province. b. Unclear relationship. c. Possibly allied with Coosa. d. Biedma says Coste is a province. e. Elvas says Ulibahali is a province. f. Garcilaso says Talisi is subject to Coosa and places it before Onachiqui; Biedma says Italisi is subject to Tascaluca.

There are no documented *entradas* into the study area after the Salas expedition of 1596 until the founding of Charles Towne in 1670. This does not mean that the Spanish were not active around the periphery of the area. The Spanish mission system was spreading all along the Georgia coast (Lanning 1935) and through northern Florida (Gannon 1965a; Geiger 1937). Intensive missionary activity began among the Potano of north-central Florida in 1600, and a permanent mission was established in 1606 (Milanich 1978:78). By 1633, missions were established in the Apalachee country of present Leon and Jefferson counties of Florida (Boyd et al. 1951). As Spanish influence spread throughout northern Florida and coastal Georgia, the Indians of the interior were undoubtedly affected. The effects are seen plainly when we get our next glimpses of the interior from the English and French in the 1670s.

When the English first reached Cofitachiqui in the interior of South Carolina in 1670 (Baker 1974), it was still a very important political unit. A letter from William Owen to Lord Ashley in September 1670 indicates clearly that the natives of Cofitachiqui were acquainted with the Spaniards. They told Owen of a land to the west, with bells and friars, which he interpreted as Spanish, and of people to the north who rode upon great deer (horses), whom Owen interpreted as Virginians (Baker 1974:IV-4).

When the Virginia traders James Needham and Gabriel Arthur penetrated the Tennessee Valley in 1673, they reported that the natives (Cherokee) were well equipped with European commodities (Williams 1928:29). They had about sixty guns, not of English make, and brass pots and kettles. From Tennessee, Gabriel Arthur traveled with the Cherokee to the South Carolina coast, where he saw Spaniards (Williams 1928:34), an indication that the Cherokee were familiar with the Spaniards. However, the guns and kettles were probably not Spanish trade goods. The guns might have been acquired from French or Dutch sources in the Great Lakes area, or perhaps they really were of English make and Arthur's denial was simply a political expedient.

At about the same time, the French were entering the Lower Mississippi Valley from the Great Lakes region. Again, we have reports of European trade items arriving ahead of the explorers at the periphery of the study area. At a point below the confluence of the Ohio and Mississippi rivers, Marquette and Joliet reported meeting an Indian group armed with muskets and possessing other European goods such as axes, hoes, knives, beads, and glass bottles (Sauer 1980:139,

141). These Indians said that the goods were obtained from Europeans on the coast some ten days away. They also found that among the Arkansas watermelons were grown (Sauer 1980:141)

In 1682, when LaSalle returned to explore the lower Mississippi, he reported finding peaches and chickens at the Arkansas villages at the mouth of the Arkansas River. Farther south, he reported, the chief of the Taensas had shields of yellow copper in his house and attendants who preceded him "carrying a sheet and round plaque of copper" (Sauer 1980:154). The "yellow copper" sounds like European brass, but the "sheet and round plaque" might be native copper.

Sauer (1980:241–43) produces adequate evidence that peaches, watermelons, and chickens were doubtlessly obtained from the Spaniards in the Southwest. The watermelon, he says, "was taken from one farming people to another ahead of Spanish advance" (Sauer 1980:241). If such European foods and other trade goods, including muskets, had reached the Lower Mississippi Valley, perhaps from the Southwest, there is little doubt that such items could just as easily have reached the study area of the interior Southeast from the relatively nearby settlements in northern Florida and on the Atlantic coast.

When LaSalle attempted to establish a colony on the Gulf coast in 1684, the Spaniards sent Marcos Delgado into the interior to investigate (Boyd 1937). Delgado provides the first glimpse of the southern portion of the study area after Tristan de Luna in 1560. He departed from San Luis (in present Tallahassee) and traveled to the northwest to the lower Tallapoosa and Coosa River area. He mentioned the Tiquipache (identified by Boyd as the Tuckabatchee; Boyd's identifications are placed in parentheses subsequently) and other groups known to be in the area in the eighteenth century. More important, Delgado listed several groups that had fled from the north "because of persecution from the English and Chichimecas and another nation called Chalaque (Cherokee). These groups included the Qusate (Koasati), the Pagna, the Qulasa of the Province of Pagna Nation, and the Tubani of the Qusate Nation and the village of Tuave which is a village of Cosate (Koasati)." It is unclear how long these people had been present in the Tallapoosa-Coosa confluence area, but Delgado mentioned the "five (chiefs or groups) that are settled and settling after fleeing from the English to the north" (Boyd 1937:21). The fact that some of the refugee groups were still settling suggests a recent arrival—a question for archaeological research.

The mention of the English to the north as well as the Cherokee and the Chichimecas (identified by Boyd as the Yuchi, following

Swanton) suggests that pressure was coming from native groups in the northern end of the Ridge and Valley province. It is even possible that the Chichimecas were the displaced Erie who later appear on the Savannah River as the Westo (Crane in Swanton 1922:291). Since the date of the inception of this pressure is unknown, it is useless to speculate. The Indian slave trade did not really begin until after the founding of Charles Towne (Wright 1981), so it is quite possible that these movements were post-1670 in origin. Delgado makes no reference to a Creek Confederacy; indeed its existence as late as 1700 has been questioned (Knight and Adams 1981:48). Using this brief historical background as a basis, we will next establish temporal divisions for the early historic period.

3

Chronology from European Trade
Goods

To measure culture change in situations where historic documentation is lacking, it is necessary to establish chronologies based on stylistic changes in categories of archaeologically recovered materials.
European-introduced trade goods have been chosen in this case for
several reasons. They were mass produced in Europe for trade all
over the world; therefore certain artifacts can serve as horizon markers over broad areas. Their worldwide incidence can provide a means
of chronological placement for otherwise undated material, in contrast to the limited usefulness of seriating local native manufactures,
for example. Whereas the interior southeastern United States includes
several regional ceramic style areas, the European goods recovered
there, coming primarily from Spanish sources, remain constant in
style (by temporal unit) across the study area. Since these European
goods were used in other parts of the world as well, they are more
likely than geographically restricted native products to be found on
archaeological sites having historically documented dates of occupation. For example, glass bead varieties found at Nueva Cadiz, Venezuela, a site of known occupation span, can be used to crossdate Indian
sites in the Southeast where they are found.

Research on European trade goods extends back to the 1930s
(Woodward 1932; Brannon 1935). Arthur Woodward was the first to
consider seriously stylistic change in trade goods as a means of chronological placement for archaeological sites. Kenneth Kidd (1954) advocated searching documents for references to goods manufactured
for trade with primitive cultures, hoping to be able to establish dates
of manufacture, but for the early period studied here, his method has

23

so far proven fruitless. The method typically employed is comparative. Either goods from sites of known date are compared with those from undated sites, or seriations based on stylistic changes are established. These techniques are not necessarily mutually exclusive. One methodology developed over the years in northeastern North America is here called the "Iroquois methodology." Its users seek to order contact period aboriginal sites chronologically by comparing the frequency of occurrence of European trade items with that of items of native manufacture. Either midden deposits or grave goods can be seriated in this manner. Sites with high frequencies of aboriginal manufactured goods and low frequencies of introduced European goods are believed to be early contact sites; over time, it is assumed, the frequency of imported European items increases and the relative frequency of native manufactured items decreases. Once a series of sites is seriated, absolute calendrical dates are assigned based upon a number of factors: approximating the length of site occupation based on the amount of accumulated midden or rebuilding of structures and, when possible, tying the sequence to historically dated events such as visits of Europeans, first evidence of missionary influence, etc. This methodology has been successfully applied to many groups including the Seneca (Wray and Schoff 1953; Wray 1973), Oneida (Pratt 1976), and Onondaga (Bradley 1979). William Fitzgerald further refined this method by assigning absolute dates to the relatively dated series of historic Neutral Iroquois sites. He examined changes in trading companies in Europe and coordinated these changes with abrupt changes in European trade items found in Neutral sites (Fitzgerald 1982:41–44). This Iroquois methodology has established estimated dates for several archaeological sites in the Northeast. While the actual calendrical dates for each site may be questioned, there is no doubt that the sites are dated correctly relative to one another, and there is little doubt that the dates assigned vary only slightly, if at all, from the actual occupation dates. These sites in the Northeast thus provide an abundance of well-dated European trade material for crossdating sites in the Southeast. The Iroquois methodology also provides a useful model for the relative dating of aboriginal sites in the Southeast if certain historical factors are considered.

In the Northeast, there was an almost constant demand for furs by Europeans. In 1524, Verrazzano found a native group in present Maine to be experienced traders (Sauer 1971:61). From then on, as European demand for furs increased, more and more European goods entered the native economy.

European contacts in the Southeast differed. The earliest contacts were usually because of the slave trade—Native Americans were captured and shipped to the Caribbean (Wright 1981:129–31). Few European goods reached the Indians in this manner, but shipwrecks along the coast of Florida provided European goods to enterprising Indian salvors and to Indians who ransomed European shipwreck victims to other Europeans. Early coastal colonizing efforts, such as those by Juan Ponce de León (1521) and Lucas Vázquez de Ayllón (1526), undoubtedly spread European goods into the Southeast, but they must have been scarce. Later expeditions, such as those of Hernando de Soto, 1539–43 (Swanton 1939), and Juan Pardo, 1567–68 (DePratter and Smith 1980), are known to have traded European goods directly in the interior. Nevertheless, until the founding of Charles Towne in 1670, there was no regular trade in furs or deerskins with the interior of the Southeast, and European goods must have been fairly rare. The possibility must be considered that Indian groups contacted by de Soto and Pardo may have obtained more European goods than their immediate descendants, so archaeological sites in the interior of the period 1540–70 may have more European goods than slightly more recent sites. The Iroquois methodology must be used with caution in the Southeast. Despite these potential hazards, though, there does seem to be a fairly steady increase in the amounts of European items reaching the Indians of the interior Southeast.

Before examining specific European trade items that are chronologically sensitive, it is necessary to consider how these items entered the aboriginal economy. Two mechanisms must be considered: direct trade by Europeans and indirect trade through native middlemen. Aboriginal trade was widespread throughout the Southeast in precontact times (Swanton 1946:736; Hudson 1976:313; Goad 1978; Walthall 1981), and European items probably reached Indian groups in the interior long before the expedition of Hernando de Soto. Indeed, members of the de Soto expedition reported finding European beads and axes in the mortuary temple at Talomeco (Bourne 1922:100); they attributed these items to the Ayllón colony of 1526. Ayllón remained on the coast, yet Talomeco is now believed to be in the South Carolina piedmont near the present town of Camden (Hudson et al. 1984). A well-organized trade in marine shells had existed throughout the Southeast since the late Archaic; it is likely that European items, probably viewed as exotic status symbols by the natives, rapidly entered this network (Smith 1975). Potentially, European items could be found anywhere in the Southeast shortly after coastal contacts began. At first these items were probably controlled by the elite as socio-technic items (Smith 1977:153).

Mary Helms has proposed a model of chiefly trade in Panama (1979). In this model, members of the elite, usually those destined to become chiefs under a system of ascribed status, went on long journeys to obtain esoteric knowledge. With the control of such knowledge, they were able to validate their status as chiefs. On their quests, they obtained exotic goods to serve as tangible displays of their new knowledge. Thus, trade in information and elite goods may have taken place via a few people moving long distances, either to the coast (perhaps accounting for the goods that de Soto saw at Talomeco) or long distances in the interior to see firsthand the European invaders. In connection with this latter possibility, it should be noted that Juan de la Bandera, scribe of the Juan Pardo expedition of 1568, reported that chiefs came from long distances to see Pardo and receive gifts (DePratter and Smith 1980:71). Using this model, it is possible to suggest that in the sixteenth century, European goods spread quickly throughout the Southeast while remaining in the hands of the elite. Visits by interior Indians to the coastal Spanish and French settlements of the sixteenth century may have been commonplace. This model of trade could account for the spread of European goods for long distances and in places not directly contacted by Europeans.

Direct trade by Europeans introduced many European objects. The U.S. de Soto Expedition Commission prepared a list of European items given to Indians (Swanton 1939:55). The later expedition of Juan Pardo gave away many European objects, especially chisels, wedges, axes, cloth, and necklaces (DePratter and Smith 1980). De Soto and Pardo traveled directly to the largest settlements that they could find, searching for wealth, food, and political alliances. Since these were the main towns of powerful chiefs, who no doubt controlled trade in elite status goods (probably including European items), it might be assumed that European items would be concentrated directly along the line of march of these expeditions. But this is not necessarily the case. During the Pardo expedition of 1568, Bandera reported that Indian political leaders came great distances to see Pardo and receive gifts (DePratter and Smith 1980:71). It is also likely that Tristan de Luna, in his colonizing effort, distributed many European items. While many of his stores were lost on the coast, Luna no doubt bartered everything that he had when starvation set in. Thus he may have traded items that were not the usual Spanish trade goods.

What happened to all this European material? It has been suggested that European items were considered wealth items (elite status goods) and were rapidly taken out of circulation. The best evidence for this theory is the mortuary deposit of Talomeco found by de Soto. European items were buried in the mortuary temple (presumably as grave goods) less than fifteen years after their arrival on the coast via the Ayllón expedition of 1526 (Smith 1976:28). European objects at the King site in northwestern Georgia appear with burials usually also accompanied by exotic aboriginal artifacts, again suggesting their role as sociotechnic status markers (Smith 1975; see further discussion in chapter 5). On the earliest sites, it appears likely that European items were quickly consumed as grave goods so they should be excellent chronological markers. There is no evidence suggesting heirlooming of such material.

Evidence from the Pardo expedition of 1568 also suggests that the aboriginal elite still controlled exotic European goods. The Pardo expedition left detailed records of the distribution of trade items. These were invariably given to chiefs, "commanders" (war chiefs?), and "principal men" (DePratter and Smith 1980:70). The only possible exception to elite control of European items was gifts to translators, whose social status is unknown.

By about 1600, however, there appeared to be a real change in the distribution of trade material, which was more abundant and did not appear to be restricted to elite burials (Smith 1977:157). This change could reflect the breakdown of powerful chiefdoms. Achieved status systems apparently were replacing ascribed status systems at least this early. European items were becoming abundant and no longer served sociotechnic functions. Iron axes, once considered elite status symbols much as were the earlier copper axes, were increasingly being used and worn out. It is possible that as this breakdown was occurring, some heirlooming of European goods may have taken place.

The possibility of heirlooming is an important consideration when using European artifacts as dating devices. There is evidence that during the mid-sixteenth century, European goods were consumed quickly as high-status grave goods; during the seventeenth century, it may no longer have been the case. It is important, therefore, to look at the total assemblage of European material at any archaeological site. It will be argued here that certain artifacts can act as "index fossils" for certain time periods, but it is always important to consider the total assemblage before assigning a date. Any artifact supplying an accurate *terminus post quem* for an assemblage must be weighed heavily when dates are assigned.

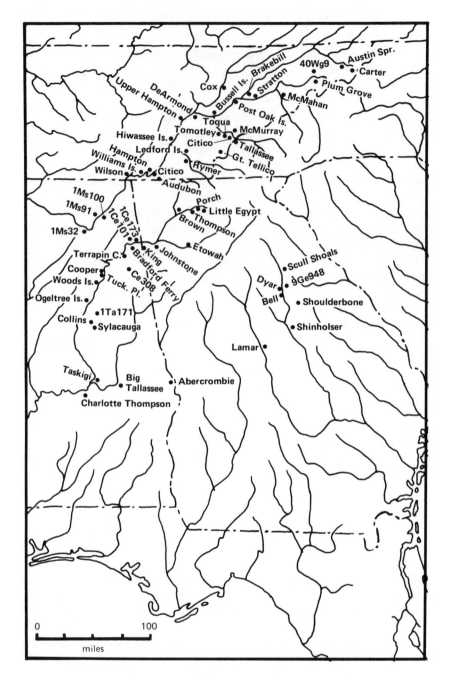

Figure 3.1. Location of archaeological sites.

Dating the artifacts

In this section we will discuss glass beads, brass ornaments, iron axes, miscellaneous hardware, and firearms. These artifact classes will be arranged in hypothesized assemblages, which will be assigned approximate calendrical ranges. This chronology will be used to measure culture change for the remainder of this study. Four temporal stages will be assigned; they represent a refinement of earlier attempts (Smith 1976, 1977). Much reliance is placed on the earlier seriation of Coosa River sites, which in turn relied heavily upon comparisons with trade material in the northeastern United States (Smith 1977). The methodology of seriating historic sites in a relatively small area has worked well for Iroquois sites, and the initial attempt at seriating sites along the Coosa River drainage in Alabama and Georgia (Smith 1977) appeared to be successful. With more evidence at hand we can refine that chronology. Archaeological sites discussed in the text are illustrated in figure 3.1.

In the earlier attempt, archaeological sites were assigned to the periods 1540–70, 1570–1600, 1600–1630, and 1630–70 (Smith 1977). The type site for the early period was the King site (Hally 1975; Smith 1975). Recent clearing operations at the site revealed a sword in a burial that was exposed by collectors. An avid student archaeologist, Keith Little, found out about the discovery and sought to identify and preserve this important find. Through his efforts, the sword is now on loan to the Etowah Indian Mounds Museum. It has been identified by Dr. Helmut Nickel of the Metropolitan Museum of Art as mid-sixteenth century (Keith Little, personal communication). The early end of the seriation is thus given a firm date.

The 1570–1600 period was represented by only one site: Terrapin Creek, 1Ce310. It was similar to the subsequent occupation at the nearby Bradford Ferry site, with an estimated occupation span of 1600–1630. Keith Little and Cailup Curren (1981) later located a site, 1Ce308, with an assemblage of trade goods clearly intermediate between those of the King site and the Terrapin Creek site. It is entirely possible that the 1Ce308 site, Terrapin Creek (just downstream from 1Ce308), and the nearby Bradford Ferry site all form a continuum of occupation by one group. The suggested dating sequence for the Coosa River is now King (1540–70), 1Ce308 (1570–90), Terrapin Creek (1590–1600), Bradford Ferry (1600–1630), Cooper Farm (1630–70), and finally Woods Island (1670–1700; reported by Morrell 1965). These dates of occupation are based on comparisons of Eu-

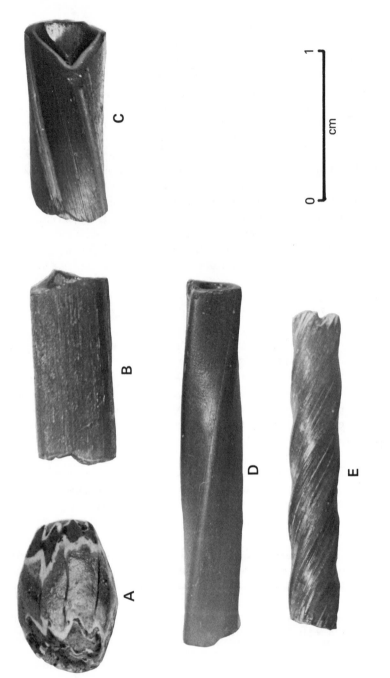

Figure 3.2. Sixteenth-century glass beads: *a*, chevron: *b–e*, Nueva Cadiz.

Table 3.1. Estimated date ranges for selected bead types

Bead type	1500	1525	1550	1575	1600	1625	1650	1675
Large Nueva Cadiz	■■■■■■■■■	■■■■■■	● ● ● ● ●					
Small Nueva Cadiz	■■■■■■■■■	■■■■■■	■■■■ ● ● ● ● ●					
Faceted chevrons	■■■■■■■■■	■■■■■■	■■■■■■	■■■ ● ● ●				
Florida cut crystal			■■■■■	■■■■■■				
Tumbled purple		■■■■	■■■					
Blue with red and white stripes				■■■■■	■■■■■			
Eye beads				■■■■■	■■■■■			
Tumbled chevrons					■■■■■	■■■■■		
Turquoise blue tumbled				■■■■■	■■■■■	■■■■	■■■■	
Amber beads		■■■■■	■■■■■					
Gooseberry	■■■■■	■■■■■	■■■■■	■■■■■	■■■■■	■■■■■	■■■■	
Turquoise blue with white stripes				■■■■■	■■■■■	■■■■		
Tumbled three-layer necklace bead			■■■■■	■■■■■				
Translucent medium blue				■■■■■	■■■■■	■■■■	■■■■	

ropean artifacts found on these sites with those from sites in the Northeast with estimated occupation dates (Smith 1977) and on the knowledge from excavated sites such as King and Bradford Ferry that occupation of the sites appears to have been of short duration. This sequence forms the basis of comparison for trade goods assemblages from other areas of the interior Southeast. Additional data on the Terrapin Creek site and the Bradford Ferry site are included in appendix 1.

Glass beads

Earlier research on trade goods has resulted in the presentation of a seriation study of glass beads from sites of the period 1513–1670 (Smith 1983). This section is based largely on that research, which will not be presented in detail. Table 3.1 lists glass beads believed to be temporally diagnostic. Using glass beads, four periods—roughly dated 1513–60, 1560–1600, 1600–1630, and 1630–70—can be recognized.

The period 1513–60 bead assemblage is made up primarily of long tubular Nueva Cadiz beads and faceted chevron beads (fig. 3.2) (Fairbanks 1968). Several additional types are present (see Smith and

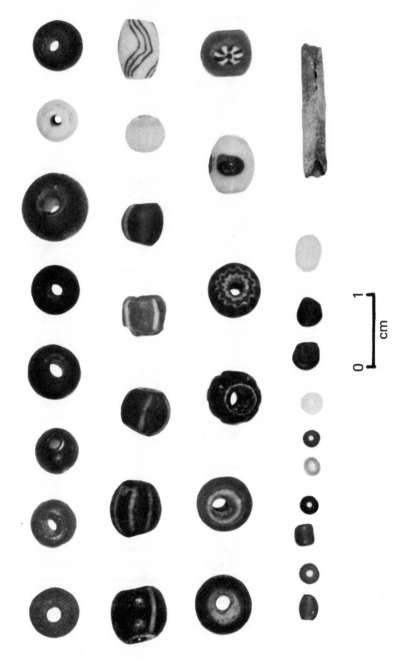

Figure 3.3. Early seventeenth-century glass beads, Bradford Ferry site.

Good 1982, for descriptions and color illustrations of beads diagnostic of this period). In the subsequent period, 1560–1600, the long tubular Nueva Cadiz types disappeared and were replaced by spherical tumbled beads—especially turquoise blue, transparent medium blue, translucent green, and navy blue beads. Faceted chevron beads were still common and some striped spherical beads appeared. A few short varieties of the Nueva Cadiz style persisted, and a few eye beads appeared (Smith 1982). Beads of cut crystal (Fairbanks 1968) and amber also occur in contexts suggesting late sixteenth-century placement (Smith 1983). Tumbled purple glass beads also occur.

The period 1600–1630 was characterized by a new style of chevron bead. The chevron bead with ground facets was replaced by a spherical, rounded chevron with green or blue exterior (fig. 3.3). Eye beads were most common during this period (fig. 3.3). Their presence represents a change from an earlier assertion that eye beads primarily dated to the last quarter of the sixteenth century (Smith 1982). New evidence from the Northeast (Fitzgerald 1982, Kenyon and Kenyon 1983) suggests that eye beads lasted into the first third of the seventeenth century, and one from the post-1606 mission of San Francisco de Potano (Florida State Museum collections; Smith 1983) substantiates a seventeenth-century placement in the Southeast. Eye beads are not known from the Apalachee missions established in 1633, so that terminal date is still considered valid. Other beads diagnostic of this period are tumbled compound beads of three layers, tumbled navy blue beads with red and white stripes, and turquoise blue beads with three or four white stripes (fig. 3.3). Seed beads are commonly of compound construction.

There appear to be no glass bead types diagnostic of the period 1630–70. Indeed, the period was remarkably free of polychrome beads. The most common beads were the common turquoise blue necklace bead, the navy blue necklace bead, and seed beads of several varieties. Eye beads disappeared, and chevron beads are unknown from the interior but are found on Apalachee missions in Florida postdating 1633. A few sites produce occasional necklace beads of types that appear to be manufactured in Holland (Karklins 1974; Bradley personal communication). They were common in the Northeast during the first half of the seventeenth century. These beads probably indicate indirect trade with English colonies to the northeast. Some of these same sites produce an occasional gun part, further suggesting indirect English contact.

Figure 3.4 Iron celts, King site.

Iron axes and knives

Iron axes and knives were always important trade items. Members of the de Soto expedition reported finding "Biscayan hatchets" in the mortuary temple at Talomeco (Bourne 1922) and an iron dagger near the fall line in Alabama (Smith 1968:242), documenting that iron tools were being obtained by aboriginal groups of the interior Southeast prior to 1540. De Soto himself distributed iron implements (Swanton 1939:55), and Juan Pardo was known to have traded some 61 chisels, 77 wedges, 72 hatchets, and 30 knives in 1568 (DePratter and Smith 1980:71). It is likely that more iron material reached the interior via aboriginal trade with sporadic European coastal visitors and, after 1565, with Spanish colonies such as St. Augustine and Santa Elena. Later the expanding Spanish mission system probably supplied some European goods for aboriginal exchange systems. Finally, the two little-known expeditions into the interior undoubtedly carried additional goods (in 1596 Salas and two friars visited Ocute, and in 1628 Pedro de Torres visited Cofitachiqui) (Swanton 1946:143).

Iron hatchets and Biscayan axes were probably small, eyed axe forms (DePratter and Smith 1980), while chisels and wedges were small, celt-like blades, probably manufactured for the Indian trade (fig. 3.4). These celt blades readily replaced the stone celts of native manufacture and probably also replaced the sociotechnic native copper axes. The de Soto expedition saw numerous copper axes at Cofitachiqui (Varner and Varner 1951:321), but they have not been found on contact period archaeological sites. Iron chisels quickly replaced them as status display items, judging from the fact that they have been found in high-status burials and also from the fact that Pardo gave out axes and chisels only to high-ranking natives.

Eyed axe forms are rare on archaeological sites of the interior predating 1630 (fig. 3.5). The only occurrence is a small hatchet from the Seven Springs site (1Ce101) on the Coosa River in Alabama (De-Jarnette et al. 1973; Smith 1977). Eyed axe forms were more common after 1630, but even through 1670 celt form iron axes were preferred. Fleming and Walthall (1978:31–32) present evidence that eyed axes were modified by native craftsmen to produce two iron celts—one from the axe blade and one from the eye, which was flattened and sharpened. The scarcity of eyed iron axes on archaeological sites prior to 1630 suggests that most were modified in this manner.

At least four major types of iron celts have been recognized: those with rectangular outline, those with trapezoidal outline, those with tri-

Figure 3.5. Eyed axe, approximately 14.2 cm long, Cooper Farm.

angular outline, and those that are round in cross section with a blade formed on one end. To date, no chronological significance has been attached to these types, although the distribution of the form with a round cross section suggests a possible association with the Tristan de Luna expedition of 1560. The small sample size hinders analysis. Iron knife blades have been found at sites that range through the complete time span being considered, but most are preserved so poorly that no meaningful typological study can be made. Occasionally other forms of iron artifacts are encountered on early contact period sites. Iron spikes are found on sites believed to date prior to 1600. Juan Pardo carried 34 pounds of nails into the interior for the construction of forts (DePratter and Smith 1980), and these should appear on Indian sites as they were no doubt quickly salvaged by the natives.

Brass ornaments

Artifacts made from European copper or brass (both designated "brass" here for ease of discussion in the face of lack of detailed analysis and to avoid confusion with artifacts of native copper) became popular trade items. Apparently brass ornaments were not constructed from worn-out brass kettles as is usually suggested for such artifacts in the Northeast. Lack of brass scrap, bail hinge fragments,

Figure 3.6. Rolled brass tinkling cones.

and bail fragments suggests that brass ornaments were produced specifically for the Indian trade by European entrepreneurs (Smith 1977). Representative "types" of brass ornaments found widespread in the Southeast also suggest European manufacture.

The earliest form of brass ornament found in the interior is the brass bead constructed from rolled sheet metal (fig. 3.6). They are occasionally found on sites believed to date to the mid-sixteenth century, but they became more popular during the early seventeenth century (Smith 1977).

Brass bracelets also became popular during the early seventeenth century. They could be manufactured either from sheet brass rolled into a tube and subsequently bent in a C shape or from a simple wide band of sheet brass with holes punched in each end to attach ties. Both types were found at the Bradford Ferry site, with an estimated date span of 1600–1630 (DeJarnette et al. 1973; Smith 1977).

Brass gorgets, either circular or (rarely) rectangular, were also popular trade items (fig. 3.7). Both shapes appear in sixteenth-century engravings of coastal Indians by De Bry (Fundaburk 1958), but such artifacts are found only on interior sites believed to date from the very late sixteenth century (Terrapin Creek, Alabama) or later. Indeed, brass gorgets were still popular at least as late as 1680 and

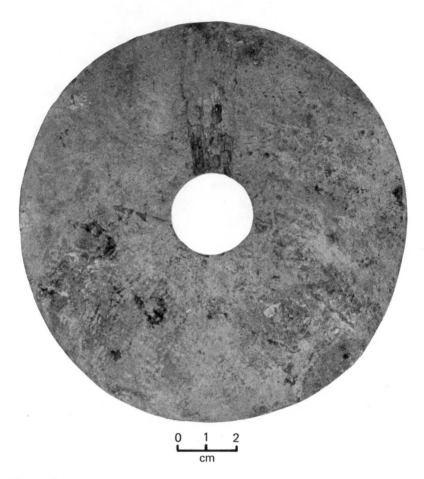

0   1   2
cm

Figure 3.7. Brass gorget, Terrapin Creek site.

probably into the eighteenth century. Since it is known that such gorgets were in circulation as early as the 1560s, some sites where they have been recovered may date to the sixteenth century. They appear to be most popular in the early seventeenth century. Sites such as Terrapin Creek (terminal sixteenth century) and Bradford Ferry (1600–1630) produce numerous examples (Smith 1977), but similar gorgets are also found on mid-seventeenth-century sites such as the Cooper Farm site (Smith 1977). A late form of brass gorget was a large, thin, crescent-shaped ornament (fig. 3.8) (Lindsey 1964:fig. 9). These occur at Cooper Farm (1630–70) and on later sites such as Woods Island (Morrell 1965). Their popularity probably peaked around 1660–90.

Brass animal effigy pendants, a form of ornament not previously studied in detail, were cut from sheet brass in the profile of an indeterminate quadruped (fig. 3.9), possibly a beaver, turtle, buffalo (Battles 1969), or even an otter. There is some variation in form: some pendants have exaggerated ears or horns (Lewis 1960), and some appear more slender than others. Table 3.2 lists known occurrences of these pendants. They are fairly widespread over the Southeast, occurring from extreme northeastern Tennessee to Mississippi. Examples have been found in the Northeast at the Blowers Oneida Iroquois site, around 1600–1630 (Bennett 1979), and at the Wilson Oneida site, around 1600–1610 (Hosbach and Gibson 1980:108–9). These are

Figure 3.8. Brass crescent gorget, 21 cm wide, Cooper Farm.

Figure 3.9. Brass animal effigy pendant, Cooper Farm.

Table 3.2. Distribution of brass animal effigy pendants

Site	Date	Reference
Settaco (Citico), Tenn.	1540–1670+	Lewis 1960
Wilson, New York	1600–1610	Hosbach and Gibson 1980
Hampton Place, Tenn.	1600–1630	Tennessee Archaeological Society 1982
Blowers, New York	1600–1630	Bennett 1979
Plum Grove, Tenn.	1600–1670	Smith n.d.
Leflore, Miss.	1630–70	Grenada (Miss.) Museum Collection
Cooper Farm, Ala.	1630–70	Smith 1977; Battles 1969
1Ms91, Ala.	1630–70	Webb and Wilder 1951
Tallassee, Tenn.	1630–90	McClung Museum Collections
1Ms100, Ala.	1630–90	Webb and Wilder 1951
Big Tallassee, Ala.	1660–1830	Auburn University Collections; Mary Elizabeth Good, pers. comm.
Ocoee, Tenn.	1690–1715	McClung Museum Collections

the earliest dated contexts for these pendants, although one from the Tallassee site in Tennessee is associated with an eye bead of a type generally out of circulation by the 1630s. Most of these animal effigy pendants seem to date to the period 1630–90, and they appear to be reliable time markers. Their widespread distribution suggests manufacture by Europeans. The earliest southeastern examples are found associated with glass beads believed to be traded by the Spaniards, while later examples appear with beads typical of those traded by the English and French (and possibly the Spaniards) after 1670. A few sites producing them also have a very few gun parts, again suggesting English contact. It could be suggested that these pendants were the result of aboriginal trade with the Spaniards in Florida (including Spanish expeditions to the Indians such as that by Marcos Delgado in 1686); however, it should be pointed out that none of these pendants has been found on seventeenth-century Spanish mission sites in Florida or along the Georgia coast or at unmissionized aboriginal sites in Florida. The possibility that they were obtained via aboriginal trade with the English in Virginia cannot be discounted, and they may have been manufactured by aboriginal craftsmen. They appear to be concentrated primarily up and down the Ridge and Valley province, a main artery of aboriginal exchange.

Firearms

Exactly when firearms were first obtained by southeastern Indians remains an important consideration for dating aboriginal sites. It is known that in 1673, when Marquette and Joliet descended the Mississippi River, they found aborigines armed with muskets (Sauer 1980: 139) in the vicinity of Memphis. The Indians said that they had acquired the firearms from Europeans on the sea coast (presumably the Gulf coast, but perhaps the Great Lakes). Similarly, when Needham and Arthur reached eastern Tennessee, crossing the Blue Ridge from Virginia in 1673, they also found the natives armed with "a bout sixty gunnes," which were not English arms (Williams 1928:29). In 1674, Henry Woodward visited the Westo on the Savannah River and found them armed with fifty or sixty guns (Swanton 1922:306). Woodward reported that the arms came from "the north," which could refer to Virginia; however, Crane (1981:6) has suggested that the Westo were a remnant of the Erie Iroquois, who were forced to flee their homes in 1654–56. If this is true, the guns could have come from the Great Lakes area and been of Dutch or French manufacture.

It is clear that native groups around the periphery of the study area were armed by the early 1670s. Can it be inferred that groups throughout the area were similarly armed? When Marcos Delgado visited the Upper Creek towns in 1686, he found refugee groups fleeing well-armed Indians in the Tennessee Valley (Boyd 1937). Apparently groups on the Coosa and Tallapoosa drainages were not well

Figure 3.10. Metal bells: *a*, Clarksdale bell; *b*, flushloop bell; *c*, cast brass bell.

armed at the time. Aboriginal warfare, mostly to obtain slaves to be sent to Charles Towne, was rampant. Indian groups quickly acquired firearms or banded together in formidable groups for protection.

There is no ready answer to the question of when southeastern natives acquired firearms. Probably some firearms were in the study area by the 1660s. By then the chiefdoms were defunct due to disease and depopulation (see chapters 4 and 5). Aboriginal patterns of acquired status had been replaced largely by a system based on status achieved by prowess in warfare, hunting, and trading. Firearms could be owned by anyone who could obtain them, and as valuable means of self-preservation, firearms were probably passed down. Most early sites with firearms parts—such as Woods Island (Morrell 1965) and some of the Guntersville Reservoir sites (Webb and Wilder 1951)—do not have firearms as grave goods; rather, gun parts are found scattered in the midden. Guns were too valuable to be buried, and parts found in the midden probably represent worn-out refuse. It is likely, therefore, that firearms were in use some time before direct evidence of them occurs on archaeological sites. Other forms of evidence, such as worn-out gun flints and lead shot, could be expected. Lead shot alone is not sufficient for dating purposes. Juan Pardo took 323 pounds of lead balls into the interior to supply his chain of forts in 1567–68 (DePratter and Smith 1980:73); these balls were no doubt salvaged by the Indians soon after the forts were abandoned. Gunflints should provide adequate evidence of the presence of firearms. It is suggested that archaeological sites in the study area producing firearms parts probably postdate the period in question, i.e., they are later than 1670. A few sites with firearms parts may date to the 1660s.

Bells

Bells can also be excellent chronological markers. A typology of trade bells has been worked out by Ian Brown (1979c). The earliest variety is the Clarksdale bell (Brown 1979c:204), a distinctive sheet brass bell, which Brain (1975) believed was associated closely with the expedition of Hernando de Soto (fig. 3.10a). While this bell form was in use in the de Soto period, we now know that it has a wider temporal distribution, lasting well into the first third of the seventeenth century (Smith 1977:156). The bell form that followed, designated the Flush-loop bell by Brown (1979c:201), first appeared during the first third of the seventeenth century (fig. 3.10b). It remained popular throughout the seventeenth and eighteenth centuries.

Finally Brown has identified several varieties of cast brass bells (1979c). He believes most of these were traded during the early eighteenth century but cites Noel Hume, who states that such bells were produced in England in the seventeenth century. Cast brass bells first appear on Seneca Iroquois sites about 1640 (Wray 1973), and they probably circulated also in the Southeast at about that time (fig. 3.10c). Bishop Calderón mentioned "Cascabeles grandes de bronce" in his letter of 1675 (Wenhold 1936:13), probably the large harness bells of cast bronze. This reference seems adequate proof that such bells were traded by the Spaniards in the seventeenth century.

Assemblages

While there are some diagnostic trade goods that can act as "index fossils" for dating archaeological sites of the early historic period, it is more important to use entire assemblages of trade materials for this purpose. Using the entire assemblage acts as a safeguard against unrecognized heirlooming and may also help provide an estimate of length of occupation. The period 1525–1670 has been divided into four assemblages (A–D) of trade materials to which have been as-

Table 3.3. European artifact assemblages

Artifact	Assemblage			
	A	B	C	D
Nueva Cadiz beads	●			
Faceted chevron beads	●	●		
Iron chisels and wedges	●	●	●	●
Clarksdale bells	●	●	●	
Tubular brass beads	●	●	●	●
Tumbled turquoise blue beads		●	●	●
Tumbled chevron beads			●	
Eye beads			●	
Eyed axes			●	●
Brass disc gorgets			●	●
Conical bangles			●	●
Flushloop bells			●	●
Brass animal effigy				●
Brass crescent gorget				●
Brass clips				●
Cast brass bells				●

signed approximate dates: A, 1525–65; B, 1565–1600; C, 1600–1630; and D, 1630–70 (table 3.3).

Assemblage A: 1525–65

Assemblage A includes types of trade goods brought in by the earliest Spanish explorers. In the interior, it would include only de Soto's goods. The later Luna and Pardo expeditions of the 1560s may have carried different merchandise to a large degree, but this possibility cannot be proven with the available historical evidence. Archaeological evidence comes from a seriation of sites and the recognition of a distinctive assemblage that is intermediate between what is designated A and C.

The best diagnostic artifact of Assemblage A is the long, tubular Nueva Cadiz style bead (fig. 3.2b, c). Historical references to these beads and archaeological evidence from historically dated early sixteenth-century sites provide accurate dating of this style (Fairbanks 1968; Smith and Good 1982). Other artifacts in Assemblage A include faceted chevron beads (fig. 3.2a), iron chisels and wedges (fig. 3.4), Clarksdale style bells (fig. 3.10a), tubular sheet brass beads (rare; fig. 3.6), and odd pieces of military hardware salvaged from the expedition of de Soto's (such as large spikes, bits of swords, armor, etc.). Eyed axe forms could be expected (fig. 3.5). One of the best diagnostic artifact forms of this period would be iron chain, but to date it has been recovered only rarely. De Soto carried much chain to enslave the Indians, and the narratives mention Indians filing off their chains to escape.

As there is good evidence that Luna and Pardo visited the same towns in the same locations as those visited by de Soto, there is a good chance that artifacts from two or even three of these expeditions might occur on the same site. It is possible that artifacts from individual expeditions might be detected. For example, the de Soto and Luna expeditions had horses, while the Pardo expedition did not. Glass bead styles are believed to have changed about the time of the Pardo expedition, and he probably traded spherical blue beads instead of the long Nueva Cadiz styles. The de Soto expedition was one of conquest, and military gear was predominant. The Luna expedition was a colonizing venture, so farming tools were no doubt common. Luna also brought several hundred Mexican farmers, and distinctive Mexican ceramics may have been carried inland. The Pardo expedition was largely a political venture in which alliances were sealed with frequent gifts (DePratter and Smith 1980). It is also probable that some new sites were established after the disruption by disease and famine of the de Soto expedition. Thus some Assemblage A sites may be short-term occupations, the King site, for example.

The forty-year interval from 1525 to 1565 we will refer to as Period A.

Assemblage B: 1565–1600

Assemblage B is virtually identical to Assemblage A except for a change in glass bead styles. The long, tubular Nueva Cadiz styles were replaced by spherical blue beads of several shades (especially turquoise blue, navy blue, and a transparent medium blue (fig. 3.3). Faceted chevron beads continue to occur and iron chisels, wedges, spikes, and Clarksdale bells are found. Eyed axes may potentially be found, although no site with this assemblage has yet produced one. Florida sites of this period produce cut crystal, silver, and amber beads, although such beads are not commonly found inland. European material is in general more common during Period B (see chapter 5.)

Sites of Assemblage B are hypothesized to represent new villages established after the first epidemics brought about by de Soto, Luna, and Pardo. Early trade material on these sites probably derives from Luna and Pardo, while later occupants of sites of this time span probably obtained trade goods from the new Spanish settlements along the Atlantic coast of Georgia, Florida, and South Carolina via aboriginal trade.

The thirty-five-year interval from 1565 to 1600 we will refer to as Period B.

Assemblage C: 1600–1630

Assemblage C is distinct from the earlier assemblages. European material is commonplace and is no longer restricted to the elite. Perhaps the best known site of this period is Bradford Ferry (Smith 1977) (appendix 1). This period had distinctive glass bead styles (fig. 3.3); the most common was the spherical turquoise blue bead introduced in Period B, but medium blue and navy blue monochrome beads were also common. The best diagnostic beads of this assemblage include chevron beads (now rounded by reheating to a spherical shape instead of being faceted on the ends), "eye beads" (Smith 1982) and tumbled compound beads of three layers. There are a great many varieties of striped beads and small "seed beads," and faceted "pony-size" beads (around 3 mm) appear in large numbers.

Iron chisels or celts are known from this period, and eyed axes also occur. The hallmark of this period is the proliferation of brass ornaments. Disc-shaped gorgets became very common (fig. 3.8), as did conical bangles, bracelets of rolled or sheet brass, and rolled tubular brass beads. The combination of the distinctive brass ornaments and particular glass bead styles is unmistakable. Clarksdale bells have been found on several sites of this period, but the first Flushloop bells (fig. 3.10b) appeared in this period. Aboriginal shell work was largely replaced by glass beads and brass gorgets.

Almost all of the trade material found in the interior at this time came from aboriginal trade with the Atlantic coastal settlements of the Spaniards. The amount of material found in the interior is unexpected, considering the absence of direct contact (except for the 1596 expedition to Ocute) and the absence of an organized deerskin trade. The Spanish mission system was well established on the Atlantic coast and was spreading into the interior of Florida to the Potano; on the other hand, Santa Elena was abandoned, and the Apalachee missions had not yet been established. Apparently aboriginal trade carried more European items into the interior than we would expect for a society on the decline. Apparently the survivors of the epidemics of the sixteenth century were now firmly established and, in the absence of direct European intervention, they were thriving in the interior. Certainly aboriginal commerce was successful.

The thirty-year interval from 1600 to 1630 we will refer to as Period C.

Assemblage D: 1630–70

Assemblage D is much like its predecessor. A number of items disappeared, including Clarksdale bells and various glass bead styles (especially eye beads, chevron beads, and multiple layer beads). Iron celts were still found, but eyed axes are increasingly common. Brass ornaments were still popular, and three new forms become important: the animal effigy pendant (fig. 3.9), the "crescent" gorget (fig. 3.8), and brass clips used to decorate leather clothing. Aboriginal engraved shell gorgets were no longer manufactured in the study area. Cast brass bells became common (fig. 3.10c); Flushloop bells were still present. While the former were no doubt manufactured in England (Brown 1979c:200), it is believed that many were traded by Spaniards. Spain was not a manufacturing center and had to purchase its trade goods from many areas (Wolf 1982:113). Cast brass bells first appear in the Northeast around 1640 (Wray 1973:23), and there is no reason

Table 3.4. Master chronology of sites of the early historic period

Site	Diagnostic artifacts	Assemblage	References	Dates
COOSA RIVER DRAINAGE				
Thompson, Ga.	Iron awl	A	Wear, pers. comm.; Muller 1966	1540–60
Brown Farm, Ga.	Iron celt	A	Smith 1977; Appendix 1	1540–60
King, Ga.	Iron celts, wedges, sword, rattlesnake gorgets	A	Smith 1975, 1977	1540–60
Little Egypt, Ga.	Nueva Cadiz bead, chisels, rattlesnake gorget, blue beads	A, B?	Smith 1979b	1540–75
Porch, Ga.	Faceted chevron, Nueva Cadiz, Clarksdale bell, sword blade, crossbow bolt tip	A	Langford and Smith 1986	1540–75
Etowah, Ga.	Iron celt	A	Smith 1977	1540–75
Ogeltree Island, Ala.	Nueva Cadiz bead, iron	A	Morrell 1964; Smith 1977; Vernon J. Knight, pers. comm.	1540–75
Charlotte Thompson, Ala.	Nueva Cadiz beads, faceted chevron beads, eye bead	A–C	Curren, Little, and Lankford 1982	1540–1630
Johnstone, Ga.	Iron celts, sword fragment, brass bead	A	Smith 1977; Appendix 1	1560–75
1Ce308, Ala.	Faceted chevron bead, blue beads iron celts, aboriginal shell gorgets, native copper	B	Little and Curren 1981	1560–90
1Ta171, Ala.	Four blue beads only	B	Vernon J. Knight, pers. comm.	1570–1600
Collins Farm, Ala.	Blue beads, possible native copper	B	Vernon J. Knight, pers. comm.	1570–1600
Sylacauga Water Works, Ala.	Chevron bead, blue beads, rattlesnake gorgets	B?	Vernon J. Knight, pers. comm.	1570–1600

Site	Artifacts		References	Date
Terrapin Creek, Ala.	Brass gorgets, faceted and tumbled chevron beads, eye beads, native shell beads	B–C	Smith 1977; Appendix 1	1590–1600
Tuckabatchee Plate site, Ala.	Iron axe, brass armbands, brass neckband, Dutch bead, buttons	D	Greer 1966, pers. comm.	ca. 1600
1Ce101, Ala.	Blue beads, Clarksdale bells, eyed axe	C	Smith 1977; DeJarnette et al. 1973	1600–1630
1Ce173, Ala.	Blue bead	C	DeJarnette et al. 1973	1600–1630
Bradford Ferry, Ala.	Flushloop and Clarksdale bells, brass gorgets, iron celts, tumbled chevron, eye beads	C	Smith 1977; DeJarnette et al. 1973; Appendix 1	1600–1630
Taskigi, Ala.	Tumbled chevron, blue beads	C	Smith 1976, 1977	1600–1630
Cooper Farm, Ala.	Eyed axes, animal pendants, brass ornaments, cast brass bells, flushloop bells, leather clips	D	Lindsey 1964; Battles 1969; Smith 1977	1630–70
OCONEE RIVER DRAINAGE				
Scull Schoals, Ga.	Navy blue bead	A or B	Williams 1984	1540–1600
9Ge948, Ga.	Eye bead, blue beads	C	Smith 1979a; Ledbetter n.d.	1600–1630
Joe Bell, Ga.	Blue beads, peach pits	C	Williams 1983	1600–1630
TENNESSEE DRAINAGE				
Austin Springs, Tenn.	Faceted chevron, iron axe	A	Polhemus 1982	1540–70
40Wg9, Tenn.	Miscellaneous iron, gold inlaid buttons	A	Smith n.d.	1540–70
Cox, Tenn.	Iron awl or spike	A	Polhemus 1982	1540–70
McMurray, Tenn.	Iron celt, brass bead	A	Smith 1976; Polhemus 1982	1540–70
Ledford Island, Tenn.	Sword blade, iron chain	A	Polhemus 1982	1540–70

(continued on next page)

Table 3.4.—*Continued*

Site	Diagnostic artifacts	Assemblage	References	Dates
Rymer, Tenn.	Horseshoe celt, musket ball	A	Polhemus 1982	1540–70
Audubon Acres, Tenn.	Faceted chevron, iron celts	A	Evans, Hood, Lautzen-heiser 1981; Smith 1976; Polhemus 1982	1540–70
Wilson, Tenn.	Copper tubular bead	A?	Polhemus 1982	1540–70
Toqua, Tenn.	Clarksdale bell, animal pendant, lugged hoe	A, D	Smith 1976; Polhemus 1982	1540–70; 1660–
Bussell Island, Tenn.	Iron celt, copper beads, blue beads, iron bracelet	A, C	Smith 1976; Polhemus 1982	1540–1630
Citico 40Mr7, Tenn.	Nueva Cadiz bead, iron celt, Clarksdale bell; various 17th-century materials	A–D	Brain 1975; Smith 1976; Polhemus 1982	1540–1670+
Great Tellico, Tenn.	Nueva Cadiz bead, cut crystal bead, blue beads, copper bead	A, B, C	Rice 1977; Polhemus 1982	1540–1800
Brakebill, Tenn.	Sword blade, blue bead	B	Polhemus 1982	1560–80
Citico 40Ha65, Tenn.	Blue beads, iron celts, brass ornaments	B	Smith 1976; Moore 1915	1560–1600
McMahan, Tenn.	Blue bead, plain majolica	B	Polhemus 1982	1570–1600
Stratton, Tenn.	Iron celt, iron spike, blue bead	B	Polhemus 1982	1570–1600
DeArmond, Tenn.	Blue beads, iron celt	B	Polhemus 1982	1570–1600
Upper Hampton, Tenn.	Blue beads, brass beads, horseshoe celt, awl, circular gorget	B	Polhemus 1982	1570–1600
Post Oak Island, Tenn.	Circular gorget, blue bead	C	Polhemus 1982	1600–1630
Tomotley, Tenn.	Brass gorget, brass bead, musket ball, blue beads	C	Polhemus 1982; Guthe and Bristline 1978	1600–1630

Site	Artifacts	Phase	Reference	Date
Williams Island, Tenn.	Eye beads, brass ornaments	C	Smith 1976	1600–1630
Hampton Place, Tenn.	Brass ornaments, animal pendants, iron celts, Clarksdale bell, iron axe	C	Tennessee Archaeological Society 1982; Smith 1976; Moore 1915; Polhemus 1982	1600–1630
Plum Grove, Tenn.	Blue beads, brass gorget, rattlesnake gorget	C, D	Smith n.d.	1600–1670
Carter House, Tenn.	Iron axe, brass gorget, blue beads, copper bead	C	Polhemus 1982	1630–70
1Ms32, Ala.	Dutch beads, brass gorgets, cast brass bells, brass clips, brass crescents, iron wedge, iron axe	D	Webb and Wilder 1951	1630–70
1Ms91, Ala.	Cast bells, animal pendant, iron axe, brass ornament	D	Webb and Wilder 1951	1630–70
Hiwassee Island, Tenn.	Brass ornaments, blue beads, seal top spoon	D	Lewis and Kneberg 1946; Polhemus 1982	1630–80
Tallassee, Tenn.	Eye bead, animal effigy pendant	C–D	University of Tennessee Collections; Richard Polhemus, pers. comm.	1630–90
1Ms100, Ala.	Brass gorget, crescent, armbands, animal pendant, cast bells, gun parts in midden	D+	Webb and Wilder 1951	1630–90
MISCELLANEOUS DRAINAGES				
Abercrombie, Ala.	Faceted chevron, blue beads, silver beads, native copper	B	Frank Schnell, pers. comm.	1575–1600
Big Tallassee, Ala.	Brass animal effigy pendant	D	Auburn University Collections; M. E. Good, pers. comm.	1660–

to doubt their simultaneous occurrence in the Southeast. By the end of this period, firearms were probably in use but were not common in the study area. Any quantity of firearms on sites in the interior Southeast generally places the sites later (after 1670). A few sites of this period produce unusual glass beads of types made in Holland and traded by the Dutch and English in areas from North Carolina northward. It is suggested that by the mid-seventeenth century aboriginal trade networks were expanded to the Northeast to obtain a greater variety of European goods. This alternative explanation may also explain the presence of British bells in the area before Carolina or Virginia explorers reached the area.

The forty-year interval from 1630 to 1670 we will refer to as Period D.

Aboriginal materials

In the Iroquois methodology we look at the ratio between aboriginally produced materials and European trade goods. Let us briefly consider the aboriginal component using the periods established by the seriation of European goods and stressing the decline of aboriginal manufacturing.

Period A is largely the pristine aboriginal period with the added European artifacts functioning in a sociotechnic mode (see chapter 5). Its sites still have native copper work—so-called Southern Cult material—although it is rare. Evidence of aboriginal stoneworking, shellworking, and ceramic manufacture shows no decline.

Period B is much like Period A, but evidence shows that native copperworking was on the decline. Sociotechnic chipped flint knives were less important, although sociotechnic forms of ground stone axes (especially the spatulate form) were still common. Shellworking was still important; beads and rattlesnake gorgets are found.

By Period C, sites no longer show evidence of working of native copper. Shell beads and gorgets are soon replaced by glass and brass counterparts. Ground stone celts are almost nonexistent, having been replaced by iron celts and eyed axes.

In Period D, there was some return to native shellworking, especially for beads and ear pins, but engraved gorgets are not found. It should be noted that there is no decline in ceramic manufacture during the early historic period. The Spaniards never traded brass kettles during the early historic period, so ceramics were as important as ever. Similarly, chipped stone projectile points remained important throughout the period, inasmuch as firearms did not become important until after 1670.

Table 3.4 lists archaeological sites in the study area that can be dated by recovered European artifacts. The dates listed are based solely to the European artifacts, although many sites dated 1540–75 had a long prehistoric occupation and some of the late sites continued to be important into the eighteenth century.

4

The Demographic Collapse

ANTHROPOLOGISTS and historians have long recognized that early European explorers introduced European and African diseases to the New World (Crosby 1972; Fish and Fish 1979; Hudson 1980; Milner 1980; Dobyns 1983). Native Americans had no natural immunity to these new diseases, and death rates soared. What in the Old World had become survivable childhood diseases, such as measles, in the New World became plagues, literally exterminating populations of New World natives. For example, the Arawaks of Santo Domingo numbered an estimated 1 million in 1492, but by 1548 only about 500 survived, according to Oviedo (Crosby 1972:45).

While historical accounts of the effects of European diseases have long existed, it is only recently that their devastating effects have been analyzed. Research by Henry Dobyns in particular has made us aware of the massive destruction of the epidemics (Dobyns 1963, 1966, 1983). Carl Sauer (1971), Alfred Crosby (1972), Suzanne Fish and Paul Fish (1979), Charles Hudson (1980), George Milner (1980), and Ann Ramenofsky (1982) have further described the process in the southeastern United States.

Historical background

What is the history of epidemic disease in the Southeast? We still do not really know, but the ethnohistorical literature provides some clues. It is, of course, possible that the first explorers who visited the Southeast introduced diseases. A single sick European could easily infect a vulnerable aboriginal group It is well documented that one car-

54

rier of smallpox who served with Cortés's conquering army was responsible for a massive epidemic in Mexico (Crosby 1972:48–49).

Ponce de León has been credited as the first European to "discover" the southeastern United States. After he explored the coast of Florida in 1513, he returned in 1521 with two hundred colonists and their livestock and horses and landed somewhere in Florida, probably at Charlotte Harbor. Indian attacks forced the colonists to retreat. Significantly, many of the colonists fell ill from an unidentified disease, which the Indians possibly also contracted (Hudson 1980).

Pedro de Salazar visited one of the barrier islands of the Atlantic coast sometime between 1514 and 1516 and contacted Indians (Hoffman 1980). In 1516, Diego Miruelo is believed to have traded with the Florida Indians for gold somewhere on the Gulf, and in 1517 Francisco Hernández de Córdova visited the same harbor previously visited by Ponce de León. In 1519, Alonzo Álvarez de Piñeda coasted the entire Gulf of Mexico from southern Florida to Panuco. He stopped at a great river, believed to be Mobile Bay, where he noted some forty villages (Swanton 1946:35). It is not known if these voyagers spread any disease, but it certainly is possible.

In 1521, Lucas Vázquez de Ayllón sent a slave-raiding expedition to the Atlantic coast; it captured several Indians. In 1526, Ayllón himself traveled to the Atlantic coast in a colonizing venture, but the colonists became ill and many died, including Ayllón. It appears likely that the Ayllón colony also was responsible for the introduction of European disease (Hudson 1980), as shall be seen later.

Pánfilo de Narváez attempted to settle Florida in 1528, but his attempts failed and a few survivors reached Mexico. Again there is specific mention of disease among Spaniards of this expedition (Fish and Fish 1979:31).

From the accounts of the de Soto expedition of 1539–43, it is clear that epidemic disease had preceded the expedition to the interior. The chroniclers of the de Soto expedition note that there had been an epidemic at Talomeco on the South Carolina fall line. According to Garcilaso, hundreds of bodies were stacked up in four of the houses. Elvas reports that several towns were depopulated and survivors had moved to other towns (in Milner 1980:43–44). Hudson notes that in the mortuary temple de Soto's men discovered European items that they believed to have come from the Ayllón colony (Hudson 1980).

In 1559, Tristan de Luna attempted to found a colony on the Gulf coast, probably at Pensacola Bay. With his food supply failing, he sent a contingent of troops inland to Coosa. Swanton (1939) and Charles

Hudson (Hudson et al. 1985) maintain that the Luna expedition reached the same Coosa town site as de Soto. If they did, it had changed: Instead of a powerful chiefdom, seven small villages are mentioned (Priestley 1928). Milner (1980:44) maintains that the discrepancy is due to demographic collapse. While generally agreeing, Hudson (1980) notes that the evidence is not as clear as he wished.

Later coastal colonizing attempts by the French and Spaniards in Florida and South Carolina in the 1560s culminated in the founding of St. Augustine and Santa Elena (Bennett 1975; Lyon 1976). Coastal mission stations were soon set up and the expeditions of Juan Pardo were sent into the interior in 1566–68, retracing a segment of the de Soto expedition from the Carolina fall line into eastern Tennessee (DePratter et al. 1983). Spanish missions were established as far north as Chesapeake Bay (Lewis and Loomie 1953). Again, opportunities for the spread of disease were many.

Once Europeans were firmly entrenched in the Southeast, historical documentation of European disease epidemics was more frequent and more reliable. In 1585, Sir Francis Drake's men contracted a highly contagious fever in the Cape Verde Islands, which Crosby believes was typhus, and they brought it to Florida when they attacked St. Augustine (Crosby 1972:40). Indians in the St. Augustine region died rapidly.

The English colony at Roanoke Island in 1587 left an impressive account of the effects of European disease on the local Indians. Thomas Hariot noted that "within a few days after our departure from everies such townes, that people began to die very fast, and many in short space" (in Crosby 1972:40; Fish and Fish 1979:32).

Later English accounts in Virginia and the Carolinas document further epidemics. John Smith in early seventeenth-century Virginia noted that for every one to two hundred Indians previously observed, only about ten remained. Smallpox epidemics are recorded for 1667 and 1696–98 (Milner 1980:46). John Lawson wrote in 1709 that smallpox had destroyed entire towns without leaving even one survivor. He estimated that only one-sixth as many Indians remained in the area as had been there fifty years earlier (in Milner 1980:46).

Spanish missionaries also dutifully recorded reduction of population due to disease in seventeenth-century Florida–Georgia. In a 1617 report, they noted that half of the missionized Indians had died in the preceding four years. Other epidemics were noted for 1659 and 1672 (Swanton 1922; Milner 1980:44). Henry Dobyns has docu-

Table 4.1. Disease epidemics in Florida, 1512–1672

Date	Disease	Probability	Mortality
1513–14	Malaria (?)	Likely	Unknown
1519–24	Smallpox	Nearly certain	50–75%
1528	Measles or typhoid	Nearly certain	About 50%
1535–39	Unidentified	Documented	High
1545–48	Bubonic plague	Nearly certain	About 12.5%
1549	Typhus	Very probably	Perhaps 10%
1550	Mumps	Possible	Unknown
1559	Influenza	Nearly certain	About 20%
1564–70	Unidentified and endemic syphilis	Documented	Severe
1585–86	Unidentified	Documented	Severe
1586	Vectored fever	Probable	15–20%
1596	Measles	Documented	About 25%
1613–17	Bubonic plague	Documented	50%
1649	Yellow fever	Documented	About 33%
1653–	Smallpox	Documented	Unknown
1659	Measles	Documented	Unknown
1672	Influenza (?)	Documented	Unknown

SOURCE: After Dobyns 1983: tables 25, 27.

mented European disease epidemics in Florida (1983); his findings are summarized in table 4.1.

Clearly there was ample opportunity for the spread of epidemic disease during the early historic period. Certainly epidemics raged in coastal areas, but did they enter the interior in general and the present study area in particular? The evidence from de Soto and the Luna expeditions suggests that they did, although Milner suggests that disease epidemics were largely geographically circumscribed within Indian sociopolitical units (1980:47). Certainly de Soto's chroniclers report evidence of disease only in the provinces of Cofitachiqui and Chalaque (Hudson et al. 1984:73).

On the other hand, it is entirely possible that pandemics swept the Southeast, a fact that Milner (1980) and Hudson (1980) consider. Henry Dobyns makes a strong case for pandemics sweeping coastal North America and suggests they spread inland as well (1983:24–25, 319). Looking at analogous situations elsewhere proves interesting.

Crosby notes that a 1518–19 smallpox epidemic in Santo Domingo could have spread to the continent before Cortés's invasion of Mexico. Smallpox has been reported in the written records of the

Maya themselves during the second decade of the sixteenth century (Crosby 1972:48).

In Peru there is good evidence that European disease preceded the Spaniards. The Inca Huayna Capac appears to have been killed, along with many of his subjects, in an epidemic, probably smallpox, in the province of Quito before Europeans landed in Peru (Crosby 1972: 51–52). It is clear that Huayna Capac had heard of the Europeans. Crosby notes, "Such is the communicability of smallpox and the other disruptive fevers than any Indian who received news of the Spaniards could also have easily received the infection of the European diseases" (1972:51). It thus seems safe to infer that Indians of the southeastern United States probably underwent multiple epidemics during the sixteenth century. Ann Ramenofsky (1982) and Henry Dobyns (1983) have argued that European disease epidemics often preceded direct European contact in North America, and Mary Helms's model (1979) of chiefly trade in Panama supports the idea that long-distance movements by traders probably ensured the rapid spread of disease vectors even across sociopolitical units.

Given the strong arguments amassed by Dobyns and Ramenofsky and the historically documented pattern of rapid spread of disease in other parts of the New World, I assume here that disease rapidly spread inland in the southeastern United States.

Documented effects of disease

Depopulation was clearly the major effect of European disease epidemics recorded in historic sources. Figures from Santo Domingo (cited previously) are no doubt representative. Henry Dobyns (1966) cites historical evidence from several New World locales to arrive at an overall depopulation ratio of 20 to 1—that is, for every twenty people in the New World in 1492, at the low point of any group's population (the times vary) only one remained. Smallpox, one of the worse killers, has a mortality rate among populations with no natural immunity of about 30 percent (Crosby 1972:44). Hudson suggests that introduced diseases such as smallpox, measles, and influenza may have killed up to 90 percent of the population (1980). Considering John Lawson's remarks that entire villages were destroyed, even that figure may not have been high enough in some areas.

In addition to depopulation, epidemic disease had many effects on the survivors. They may have been weakened enough to die later of starvation (Crosby 1972:47; Fish and Fish 1979:32), especially if everyone was sick at critical times of planting or harvest and subsistence activities were thus interrupted.

Social and political relations were also affected by epidemic disease. Crosby discusses the effects of disease on the Aztec power structure (1972:54). As the leaders were struck down by disease, the processes of government were disrupted and conquest by the Europeans was assured. Milner notes that the long-term effects of disease "attributable to an insufficient labor force, including specialists, probably necessitated societal reorganization and coalescence of formerly discrete groups in order to remain as viable social and economic entities" (1980:47). Such population movements are well documented. In such a reorganization in Amazonia during the twentieth century, surviving Sabane "have joined forces with survivors of other Nambikwara groups, so an amalgam social unit may eventually survive" (Dobyns 1966:413). Banding together of survivors then was one response to epidemics. Another was flight, the best account of which is that of the Gentleman of Elvas. Discussing the effects of disease on the province of Cofitachiqui in piedmont South Carolina just east of the study area, Elvas reported that plague survivors removed to other towns (Smith 1968:63; Milner 1980:43). Clark Wissler (in Dobyns 1966:441) reports a shift in tribal territory following a 1780 epidemic that swept western North America, a shift resulting from differential survival. The Cakchiquel Mayas of Guatemala, in their own record of an epidemic of 1520–21, noted that half of the people fled (Crosby 1972:58). Dobyns discusses simplification of social systems and settlement shifts as a response to disease (1983:313–28).

Perhaps the most serious effect of epidemic disease is an overall loss of elements of culture. Charles Hudson (1980) cites Akiga, a Tiv, who told of depopulation so swift and so devastating that ancestral traditions were lost. Hudson suggests that such was the case in the Southeast: "We can be sure that our understanding of southeastern Indian knowledge, philosophy, religion, and art symbolism is the merest fragment of what existed at the time of de Soto's *entrada*." Bruce Trigger (1976:601) similarly suggests the loss of much traditional religious lore among the Huron following the epidemics of the 1630s. The loss of religious and genealogical lore to a traditional aboriginal group must not be underestimated: It is an important factor in culture change, and it surely paves the way for acculturation. Hudson (1980) further suggests that a heavy loss of life in the chiefly lineage "would probably have led to the segmentation of chiefdoms into several smaller, less centralized social entities."

The historical record documents several results of epidemic European diseases that can be expected to have occurred in the southeastern United States: massive depopulation, population movement, social and political reorganization, and loss of many elements of culture.

Archaeological parameters

It is clear from historical accounts and work by ethnologists and ethnohistorians that European epidemic disease had a devastating effect on the New World, but few anthropologists have made an effort to correlate these historically known phenomena with the archaeological record. Can archaeological data be used to fit the model of drastic population decline? Some of the hypotheses offered in the remainder of this chapter can be tested with available data; others will require further research.

Skeletal remains might seem to hold the most obvious evidence of the effects of European-introduced epidemic diseases. Those diseases, however, were usually quick killers in newly contacted populations and left little evidence on bones (Milner 1980:49). Bones of survivors may show the formation of Harris lines or enamel hypoplasia, but these are simply markers of stress and cannot be correlated positively with specific diseases (Milner 1980:49). Such stress markers might also be associated with famine—which may or may not be a secondary result of epidemic disease (Fish and Fish 1979:32; Milner 1980:47).

Hudson (1980) suggests that the first epidemics may have been so devastating that no one was left to bury the bodies. The historical accounts of epidemic disease suggest that a few people always survive; however, it is possible to believe that sometimes bodies were left exposed before burial. In such a case, several pieces of evidence could be hypothesized for the archaeological record. Bones left exposed might show gnawing marks from dogs or rodents, but, to my knowledge, no such marks have been reported in the literature. Only disarticulated or partially disarticulated remains might be available for later burial; portions of the body might have been removed by scavengers. Recent research by David Mathews on the King site skeletal series indicates that there is evidence of gnawed bones. Seckinger (1975:67) notes missing skeletal elements, but it is not clear whether lack of preservation, delayed burial, or some other factor is to blame.

Burial at a later date might take the form of a "mass" burial (i.e., more than two bodies) (Milner 1980:48). Milner cautions that, because mass burial may be the result of other factors such as retainer sacrifice, the context of mass graves must be considered carefully. Mass burial was not common in the prehistoric Southeast; however, at the sixteenth-century King site a mass grave was found that would appear to be a strong candidate for a postepidemic burial. The Period A and D Toqua site excavated by Richard Polhemus for the University of Tennessee's Tellico Reservoir project contained three mass burials of three, five, and seven individuals, again suggesting European disease (Richard Polhemus, personal communication). Other evidence of depopulation at Toqua will be considered below. Mass burial grave features should be encountered on other early sites when they are excavated.

Milner suggests that "multiple" burials (i.e., exactly two bodies) could also be expected to result from European disease epidemics (see fig. 4.1). There is historical documentation that multiple burial can be the result of European epidemic disease. Describing the Arkansas in 1698, St. Cosme noted, "Not a month had elapsed since they had rid themselves of smallpox, which had carried off most of them. In the village are now nothing but graves, in which they were buried two together, and we estimated that not a hundred men were left" (Kellogg 1917, quoted in Philips et al. 1951:410).

There does appear to be a rapid increase in multiple burials in the study area during the sixteenth century (Periods A and B). Again, the King site provides the best documented examples: 9 of 210 burials at the site were multiple burials (Hally 1975; Seckinger 1977).

In eastern Tennessee, Lewis and Kneberg note, multiple burials were numerous on sites of the Mouse Creek culture: "In numerous instances two bodies had been interred at the same time, one directly superimposed above the other, usually both individuals being of the same sex. There is little likelihood that the second body was placed in the grave at a later time than the first since the bones were in actual contact and often without the slightest trace of soil between the points of contact" (1941:8). Both the Ledford Island and Rymer sites, which have been assigned to Period A, are Mouse Creek sites, as is Upper Hampton Place, which is from Period B.

Available data on mass and multiple burials are summarized in

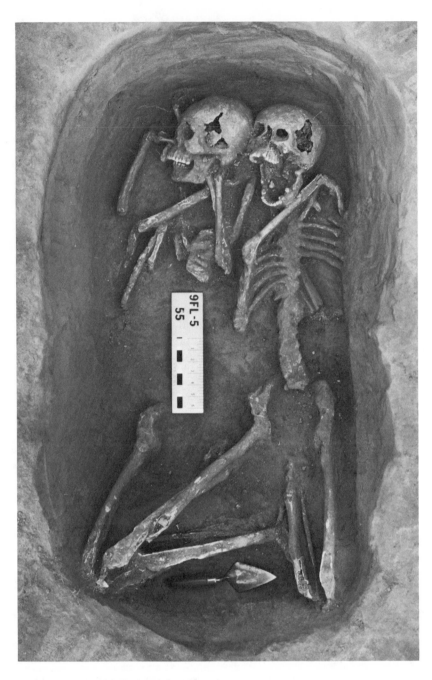

Figure 4.1. Multiple burial, King site.

table 4.2. Unfortunately, there are biases in these data. Several of the sites have long, prehistoric occupations; if these burials measure the frequency and extent of European disease epidemics, then earlier prehistoric individual graves dilute the findings. It is also possible that victims of particularly horrible epidemics may have been disposed of in some other fashion than the normal village burial.

The King site, occupied for less than fifty years (Hally 1982), probably all within Period A (1525–65) (including a possible prehistoric founding), provides probably the best data for the evaluation of European disease epidemics. While only 6 percent of the graves were mass or multiple burials, these graves account for at least 15.5 percent of the people. This percentage may not seem high when up to 90 percent may have been affected by an epidemic disease, but it must be remembered that there is no reason to expect that all victims received multiple or mass burial.

Data from Period B (1565–1600) are hard to find. While site 1Ce308 has a high frequency of mass and multiple burials, its low sample size makes the figure suspect. A better sample from Upper Hampton Place suggests that disease became less a problem in the late sixteenth century after Spanish exploration was over. Clearly, more data are needed.

Period C (1600–30) again shows evidence of mass and multiple burials. Both Bradford Ferry and Tomotley appear to be single component sites, and they have fairly large samples of burials. Again, the interpretation may be put forward that disease was a problem in the early seventeenth century, precisely the period that sees a tremendous influx in European goods. Ramenofsky (1982:257) noted that smallpox virus can be transmitted in a dry state on objects; thus anyone coming into contact with European goods could be exposed to smallpox.

Period D (1630–70) appears to be relatively disease-free, judging from the lower frequency of mass and multiple burials. Clearly more data are needed for all these periods. It is possible that mass and multiple burials are not directly associated with European epidemics but are the result of another event.

Recent reanalysis of the King site skeletal series under the direction of Robert Blakely of Georgia State University has produced another interpretation of mass and multiple burials. At least one person in each mass or multiple burial appears to have been the victim of a battle with Europeans, probably from the de Soto expedition. The

Table 4.2. Frequency of mass and multiple burials

Site	Number of burials	Number of mass graves	Number of multiple graves	Mass plus multiple (percent)	Reference
Period A (1525–65)					
King	213	4	9	6.1	Hally 1975
Ledford Island	459	6	16	4.8	McClung Museum notes
Rymer	168	0	6	3.6	McClung Museum notes
Toqua[a]	433	3	6	2.1	Richard Polhemus, pers. comm.
Citico 40Mr7[a]	194	0	0	0.0	Richard Polhemus, pers. comm.
Citico 40Ha65[a]	106	0	1	0.9	Moore 1915
Period B (1565–1600)					
1Ce308	14	1	0	7.1	Little and Curren 1981
Upper Hampton	56	0	1	1.8	McClung Museum notes
DeArmond Village[a]	52	0	0	0.0	McClung Museum notes
Period C (1600–1630)					
Bradford Ferry	47	1	1	4.3	DeJarnette et al. 1973; Appendix 1
Tomotley	92	1	7	8.7	Guthe and Bristline 1978
Hampton Place	31	0	0	0.0	Moore 1915
Period D (1630–70)					
1Ms100	74	1	1	2.7	Webb and Wilder 1951
1Ms32	68	0	0	0.0	Webb and Wilder 1951
1Ms91 Unit 1	56	0	1	1.8	Webb and Wilder 1951
Cooper Farm	25	0	0	0.0	Lindsey 1964; Battles 1969, 1972; Humbard and Humbard 1965

a. Includes prehistoric component.

types of wounds and their locations on the body indicate that the trauma was inflicted by metal weapons in a manner consistent with warfare in medieval Europe (Mathews 1984). However, only some of these wounds were fatal; many healed (Blakely, personal communication).

One of the goals of this skeletal reanalysis was to look for evidence of epidemic disease. Robert Blakely (personal communication) states, "In theory at least there is room for both European disease and trauma among King's decedents. However, Koener's and my exhaustive search for epidemic disease at the site has failed to turn up any evidence for Spanish-introduced diseases. The bones show no lesions indicative of smallpox, typhus, measles, etc. (Statements to the contrary notwithstanding, these diseases do occasionally produce skeletal symptoms.) Concerning demographic structuring, one would anticipate elevated mortality in the 4- to 18-year-old age category as a result of European diseases. (The reason is that such diseases, again contrary to oft-stated opinion, do not preferentially affect the aged and very young; under lack of immunity conditions, morbidity shows no favorites. Therefore, the typically healthiest segment of the sample should show the greatest mortality in contrast to nondiseased populations.) King actually evidences lowered mortality in that age group when compared with prehistoric samples. . . . The bottom line is that there is no direct or indirect evidence that European diseases visited the King site. That does not, of course, mean that they were absent."

The King site data are thus inconclusive. Apparently, some of the multiple-burial decedents were casualties of warfare, perhaps a European-Indian confrontation; some whose wounds healed clearly died well after the trauma. Others exhibit no wounds and may have been disease victims. The fact that some "battle victims" were interred in multiple graves confirms that such a mode of burial was not reserved for epidemic disease victims. Yet multiple burials occur from central Tennessee to central Alabama. Certainly, de Soto did not eliminate such a large quantity of natives. Aboriginal warfare is, of course, a possibility, but an interpretation encompassing all explanations is also feasible. Perhaps multiple and mass burials were used for victims of either war or disease.

Urn burial and bundle burial may also reflect the presence of European disease epidemics. These secondary forms may have been adopted when there were not enough healthy individuals to bury the victims of epidemic diseases promptly and more conventionally.

Urn burial has a long history; it definitely occurs in the study area in the prehistoric period. It was common for children during the

Early Dyar phase (about 1450–1500) in the Oconee River drainage (Smith 1981). By the time of European contact, urn burial was no longer practiced in the Oconee area, but it became important along the western margin of the study area at precisely the period under discussion. The Alabama River phase, located along the margins of the Alabama River and up the Black Warrior drainage, used urn burial as a common treatment of the dead (Sheldon 1974). European trade goods are found in urn burials occasionally, allowing a dating to Period C (Curren 1982:107). There is little doubt that the Alabama River phase was primarily a seventeenth-century phenomenon.

A similar practice (without the pottery vessels) is reflected in the bundle burials of the Tennessee River area. The best reported series of bundle burials comes from the Hiwassee Island site (Lewis and Kneberg 1946:150–51). Lewis and Kneberg date all Hiwassee Island burials with trade goods to the early eighteenth century, but the trade materials illustrated in their plates 86–88 appear to date from the period 1650–1700, or Period D and later. The brass discs, lugged hoes, seal top spoon, brass tubular beads, and some of the glass beads seem to be diagnostic of the seventeenth century. Lewis and Kneberg report European objects with both flexed and bundle burials. The flexed burials seem to date to Period D, the bundle burials slightly later but perhaps still in the terminal portion of Period D. That the urn reburials of the Alabama River and the bundle reburials of the Tennessee River reflect seventeenth-century responses to European disease epidemics is a hypothesis worth pursuing.

What other evidence for early European contact might be expected from burial analysis? Perhaps the most obvious would be the burial of a European. Such a find would not be unexpected, given the number of people who died on the de Soto and Luna expeditions. Burials of mixed European (or African) and Indian genetic types should also be expected on sites of the early historic period. To date, no such burials have been found (or recognized) within the study area, but one has been recognized from the Georgia coast (Zahler 1976:27–28, 50–51) and another from the early seventeenth-century Neutral Iroquois Grimsby site in Canada (Kenyon 1977, 1982:39). Most of the skeletal series from sites of the early historic period have not been analyzed by physical anthropologists.

Another analysis of burial data for indications of European disease involves looking at population curves for large skeletal series. Such analysis has been advocated by Milner (1980) and Hudson (1980).

Since disease is hardest on the very young and very old, these age groups would be represented disproportionately in an epidemic mortuary series. There is even some evidence that adolescents and young adults would also be affected to a greater degree than the remainder of the population (Milner 1980:49). Such analysis requires a large skeletal series. To date only the King site sample of 213 burials has been analyzed; it showed an unusual population curve suggestive of European epidemic disease (Hally 1975:34; Tally 1975). However, reanalysis by Gary Funkhouser (1978) disputed Tally's conclusions. The major reanalysis of the King site skeletal series currently being conducted by Robert Blakely should help resolve the dispute. He notes (personal communication) that the population curve is unusual, but it does not seem to indicate epidemic disease.

While analysis of burials might offer the best opportunity for studying the effects of European disease, it is clear that these data have not been developed to any extent. Fortunately, other archaeological parameters enable us to seek out the effects of European epidemic disease and depopulation over time. These include site size, number of sites, and population movement (Hassan 1981; Ramenofsky 1982).

The idea that sites would become smaller and fewer over time as population is reduced is obvious, but measuring such changes must be done cautiously. It is clear from the ethnohistorical literature that much population movement was taking place during the late part of the early historic period. The effects of such movements and the banding together of refugee groups must be taken into consideration. A model of the expected changes in settlement might be expressed as follows.

In the period around initial contact (including the pre–de Soto interior), populations would be expected to decline rapidly (Ramenofsky 1982). New sites established during this period by people fleeing disease areas might be considerably smaller and for at least a limited time should grow smaller and smaller. When town populations reach a certain low limit, population movement and the possible regrouping of populations could be expected to take place. Milner (1980:47) has noted that long-term effects of European epidemic disease and ensuing famine would lead to an insufficient labor force, including specialists, and would probably necessitate the reorganization of society and the coalescence of formerly discrete groups in order to remain viable social and economic entities (see also Dobyns 1983:303). Thus there should be a detectable population movement and a decrease in the number of sites through time. It now remains to determine appropriate archaeological measurements of this hypothesized process.

Site size

Site size is a recognized parameter of population size (Hassan 1981: 66–72; Ramenofsky 1982). Certainly site size can be simply measured, but a number of factors must be considered. A village's size can fluctuate over time, growing larger or smaller and varying with many factors other than European disease. Since we are interested not in the extent of a site but in its population, the best approach would be to count the number of houses in a site and multiply that number by an estimated family size (Hassan 1981:72). Another estimate that can be made from the archaeological record is to measure the floor area of domestic structures and estimate the population using Raoul Naroll's figure of one person per ten square meters of floor area (1962). For purposes of comparison, Naroll's is probably the most accurate means of estimating population, but it requires extensive archaeological excavations to determine the number of houses present on a site contemporaneously and their dimensions. Such data are available only for the King site (table 4.3) and only for approximately one-half of it. Assuming the unexcavated half to mirror the excavated half (Hally 1975), we can estimate a population (rounded) of three hundred for the King site, which has a habitation area of 138,300 square feet (calculated from figures in Hally 1975), not including the central open plaza. This method yields a figure of 461 square feet of habitation area per person in the village overall. It could be argued that this figure reflects a normal proximic situation for this specific archaeological culture (Barnett phase) or this ethnohistorically known province (Coosa). Making this assumption, it will be possible to estimate populations for a number of other sites when site size and sacred precinct size (plaza and mound area) are known. The estimated population will equal the total site size minus the plaza size (which equals the habitation area) divided by the constant 461 square feet per person. Table 4.4 presents such data for sites believed to be closely related politically to the King site.

A cruder measurement, but useful when sacred precinct area is unknown, is the overall area of site per person. Again, using the King site data as the base (220,800 divided by 300), we calculate one person to about 736 square feet of total site area. This cruder figure will allow us to measure additional sites (table 4.4). This estimate is considered less diagnostic because the relationship of habitation area to sacred

Table 4.3. King site structure data

Structure number	Dimensions (in feet)	Area (in m²)	Total population (at 1 per 10 m²)
1	32×32	95.13	9
2	27×29	72.74	7
3	20×22	40.88	4
4	18×18	30.10	3
5[a]	24×27	60.20	6
6	25×25	58.06	5
7	21×22	42.92	4
8	27×26	65.22	6
9	24×24	53.51	5
10[a]	26×30	72.46	[7]
11	26×21	50.73	5
12	26×26[b]	62.80	6
13	30×31	86.40	8
14	27×29	72.74	7
15	29×31	83.52	8
16[c]	21×20.5	39.99	
17[c]	49.5×49	225.3	
18	21×20	39.02	3
19	21×23	44.87	4
20	21×23	44.87	4
21	30.5×30	85.01	8
22	25×24	55.74	5
23	29×31	83.52	8
24	32.5×27	81.52	8
25	24×30	66.89	6
26	27×27	67.73	6
27	31×31.5	90.72	9
28	21×21	40.97	4
			148

a. Only structure 5 or 10 occupied at same time.
b. Incomplete excavation.
c. Not a domestic structure.

precinct area is not known and may not be linear. Politically important towns may have had a proportionally larger sacred precinct than did sites farther down the hierarchy.

While there are few data for comparison, the two Period A sites, Etowah and Little Egypt (probably the towns of Itaba and Coosa, respectively), that have long prehistoric occupations and multiple mounds are larger than sites that probably originated during the historic period, such as the King site. It is possible that the King site

Table 4.4. Site size and population data: Coosa province

Site	Site size (sq. ft.)	Sacred precinct	Habitation area	Habitation population[a]	Site area population[b]	Reference
Period A (1525–65)						
King	220,800	82,500	138,300	300	300	Hally 1975, 1982
Little Egypt	600,000[c]	126,400	473,600	1,027	815	Hally 1980:8
Etowah	2,265,120[c]	295,425	1,969,695	4,273	3,078	Larson 1972
Audubon Acres	152,460[d]	–	–	–	207	Evans, Hood, Lautzenheiser 1981
Ogeltree Island	200,000	–	–	–	272	Alabama site files
Citico 40Mr7	111,000	3,200	107,800	234	151	Richard Polhemus, pers. comm.
Rymer	210,000	–	–	–	285	McClung Museum files
Toqua	180,000[c, e]	26,250	153,750	334	245	Richard Polhemus, pers. comm.
Brown Farm	390,000	–	–	–	530	Appendix I
Period B (1565–1600)						
Upper Hampton	476,000	–	–	–	647	McClung Museum files
DeArmond (village)	315,000[c]	–	–	–	428	McClung Museum files
Period C (1600–1630)						
Bradford Ferry	70,000	–	–	–	95	DeJarnette et al. 1973
Tomotley	135,000[c]	–	–	–	183	Guthe and Bristline 1978
Period D (1630–70)						
1Ms100	45,000	–	–	–	61	Webb and Wilder 1951
1Ms32	264,000	–	–	–	359	Webb and Wilder 1951
After Period D						
Woods Island	180,000	–	–	–	245	Morrell 1965

a. At one per 461 square feet. b. At one per 736 square feet. c. Prehistoric occupation present; size of historic component unknown. d. 3.5 acres. e. Latest.

simply is lower in a hierarchy of sites, but other sites occupied during the historic period, such as Audubon Acres and Ogeltree Island, are of similar size. Data are not available to permit determining whether these sites originated during the early historic period or had long occupations. With current data we can only suggest a trend toward smaller sites. Later sites, such as the Period C Bradford Ferry site, are considerably smaller.

Some sites do not appear to fit the hypothesized pattern. The exact culture history of the Upper Hampton Place site is not known. It may or may not have a long prehistoric component. Its long, thin settlement area may indicate a transition to the dispersed settlement type discussed below, but the site does have a series of palisade ditches. Its large population estimate (table 4.4) remains anomalous. The De-Armond village site definitely has a long prehistoric occupation, so the total site size may not have any bearing on the area occupied in Period B. The site size for Citico, 40Mr7, seems too small for a mound center (its reported size is the best estimate available: Richard Polhemus, personal communication). There is some archaeological evidence that Citico was first occupied in Period A, so perhaps the small size reflects early epidemics. Finally, 1Ms32 appears to be a large site with a high population; but it is a dispersed linear settlement, and there is no reason to believe it was as densely populated as the earlier palisaded towns (see discussion below).

The Toqua site deserves special mention, since it was excavated carefully during the University of Tennessee's Tellico Reservoir project (Schroedl and Polhemus 1977; Richard Polhemus, personal communication). This Dallas mound center was occupied from around 1215 to 1620 (based on radiocarbon dates from mound A) and was carefully fortified by palisades. Interestingly enough, the size of the site shrank during its life span. The earliest village covered some 420,000 square feet with houses neatly dispersed. Later the occupied area shrank to 210,000 square feet, and houses were densely packed into the fortified area. This reorganization of the settlement took place between 1350 and the sixteenth century. Then (perhaps 1580–1600, according to Polhemus) the fortified area shrank again, to 180,000 square feet; in this area are all the burials containing European trade goods (both Periods A and D). All three mass burials excavated were within this last palisade, strengthening the argument that they represent victims of European disease epidemics. Mound B is excluded by this last palisade. It should be noted, however, that two of the six multiple burials fall outside of this latest palisade line. The overall impression is that, after the initial reorganization of Toqua settlement into a densely nucleated town of the size of the King site, there was further shrinkage perhaps due to disease (the mass burial evidence). Clearly the site was on the decline, because mound B was abandoned. The evidence from trade goods, both types and scarcity, suggests that Toqua was abandoned in the sixteenth century. The Period D occupation probably signals the arrival of the Cherokee in the valley during the last quarter of the seventeenth century.

Number of sites

Another obvious measure of depopulation would be a decrease over time in the number of sites occupied. Interestingly, the number of sites occupied at one time is not considered by Hassan (1981) as a measure of population, probably because he does not adopt a regional approach. Ramenofsky (1982), to the contrary, does consider settlement counts as a method of measuring population decline. If only a small area is looked at with this measurement in mind, then it must be strongly considered that population movement (migration) could be an explanation for any observed decrease in the number of sites. If areas as large as the study area are considered as a whole, then the effects of migration should be minimized. Ramenofsky advocates such a regional approach. Table 4.5 presents data by drainage system and as totals for the western study area (Coosa and Tennessee River drainages). In both of these drainages, there is a decrease in the number of sites from Period A to Period B followed by a stabilization or increase from Period B to C and a subsequent decrease to Period D. There is no evidence that populations were living in small hamlets or farmsteads in the Tennessee Valley either in the late prehistoric or early historic periods (Richard Polhemus, personal communication). The data in table 4.5 might be interpreted as follows: major European disease epidemics reduced populations during Period A; by Period C,

Table 4.5. Decrease in number of sites in western study area

	Period A 1525–65	Period B 1565–1600	Period C 1600–1630	Period D 1630–70
Coosa River drainage	9	7	6	2
Tennessee River drainage	12	8	10	8
Miscellaneous drainages	–	1	–	1
Totals	21	16	16	11

populations were stabilizing or even growing to some extent; by Period D, the number of sites again diminished, perhaps reflecting the beginning of population consolidation and the beginning of the Creek Confederacy, as well as renewed contact with Europeans.

The Wallace Reservoir provides additional data. Few Wallace Reservoir sites have produced European trade goods, primarily due to lack of extensive excavations. Nonetheless, a detailed ceramic chronology has been established (Smith 1981), and radiocarbon determinations and some European trade goods provide tight chronological controls.

Explorations in the Wallace Reservoir have located approximately 800 Mississippian sites (Rudolph and Blanton 1980:14), ranging in size from large towns to small special-purpose sites, an unusually large sample. The largest site (229,273 square feet), the Dyar mound and village, was occupied from approximately A.D. 1000 to 1550 (Smith 1981) and is the type site for the Dyar phase, an archaeological construct overlapping the period of early Spanish exploration. The Dyar site may well be the Cofaqui of the de Soto chronicles, as discussed previously. It shows gradual decline and abandonment during the sixteenth century, suggesting the effect of European disease (Smith 1981:256).

The subsequent indigenously developed occupation of the reservoir is the Bell phase. The largest known site of the Bell phase (65,340 square feet), Joe Bell, 9Mg28, is the type site for the phase (Williams 1981). The Bell site has produced European trade materials and radiocarbon determinations (Williams 1981) that date it to Period C. Comparing the largest sites, we observe a reduction in site size from the Dyar phase to the Bell phase, which suggests drastic population decline.

To study more closely the effects of disease on the Wallace Reservoir area, a large sample of sites was investigated for data on the number and size of components of the Late Dyar and Bell phases. This sample consisted of four transects, which were selected to cross the reservoir area in specified ecological niches. Both broad alluvial valley uplands and narrow valley shoals areas were selected as sample strata (Siegel n.d.). Within these strata, 253 Lamar period components were recognized (see appendix 2 for ceramic dating methodology): 101 were Late Dyar phase components (sixteenth century) and 63 were Bell phase components (seventeenth century). Since the durations of these phases are for all practical purposes identical (a minimum of fifty years and a maximum of one hundred years by current estimates

[Smith 1981; Williams 1983; Gary Shapiro, personal communication]), these two phases will be considered directly equivalent temporal units. Differences between the settlement of these two phases can be attributed to the effects of European disease or migration. Since no heavy Bell phase occupation is known outside the Wallace Reservoir area, the migration explanation appears unlikely.

Are there differences between the settlement of the two phases? It is obvious that numbers of sites decreased dramatically from 101 to 63, but what about site area? In order to test for differences in site area, it was necessary to remove multicomponent sites from consideration since the size of each individual component was not calculated by Wallace Mitigation Survey personnel. Indeed, such identification would have been impossible, since the phase designations utilized here were developed in the laboratory after the survey was completed. The removal of multicomponent sites results in a sample consisting of 38 Bell phase sites and 80 Late Dyar phase sites. Site area had been calculated in the field (David J. Hally, personal communication), and these figures were compared with a T test (SPSS = X Release 2.0). A two-tailed test was used on the hypothesis that mean site size for each phase was equal. Even though the mean site size for the Bell phase was only 4,648.4 square meters compared to 6,807 square meters for the earlier Late Dyar phase, the T test indicated that these sizes were not significantly different (T = 1.08; DF = 116; significant only at 0.285 level). How is this lack of difference to be interpreted?

The largest single component site of the Late Dyar phase in the transects covered 61,286 square meters, the largest Bell phase site 42,394 square meters. There were fifteen Late Dyar phase sites with areas over 10,000 square meters compared to only five Bell phase sites of this size, indicating that the larger sites were dropping out of the settlement hierarchy (at least few large sites were established during the Bell phase).

Nonetheless the T test indicates that mean site size is not significantly different in the two phases. The likely explanation is that both phases have large numbers of smaller sites that are about the same size. While there is a great decrease in numbers of sites, it is apparent that an attempt was made to maintain certain site size units for economic or social reasons or both. The Bell phase survivors of epidemic disease probably regrouped into basic socioeconomic units that were approximately the same size as units of the Late Dyar phase. Thus site size remained roughly constant, but numbers of sites decreased dramatically. This interpretation fits the historically expected processes described by Milner (1980:47) discussed earlier. Dobyns also discusses the notion of a culturally defined model of a proper settlement size (1983:303). Ramenofsky (1982:267) notes that "Residential instability and/or village reduction coupled with amalgamation processes which occur when the population of villages falls below a threshold necessary for defense and maintenance are attempts to maintain adaptations that developed when the population base was much larger." This process is hypothesized as the best explanation of the Wallace Reservoir data.

Population movement

Another historically documented effect of European disease is population movement. Two types are mentioned in the documents: rapid flight from areas of epidemic disease and slower movements brought about as tribal balances of power shift with changing demography.

As we understand the earliest Spanish explorers, there is not much evidence of rapid flight from sites in the study area because of disease. While the de Soto narratives mention the abandonment of Talomeco just east of the study area, interpretations of the routes of de Soto, Luna, and Pardo by Charles Hudson and his associates (DePratter et al. 1983, 1985; Hudson et al. 1984, 1985) indicate that the later Luna and Pardo expeditions visited the same towns as de Soto. It is possible that these towns were abandoned for short periods and then subsequently reoccupied, but this premise would be difficult to demonstrate archaeologically.

What can be demonstrated, at least in some portions of the study area, are gradual population movements. It is assumed that these movements were the result of European disease since a great deal of residential stability can be demonstrated in the study area prehistorically. Some major mound centers were occupied for hundreds of years (see chapter 5 and table 5.1). It is possible, of course, that other factors caused population movements.

The Coosa River drainage provides the best evidence for gradual population movement. It is an area in which intensive archaeological research has taken place (Morrell 1964, 1965; Wauchope 1966; DeJarnette et al. 1973; Smith 1977; Little and Curren 1981; Curren et al. 1982; and data gathered from several private collectors), and it can comfortably be assumed that there is a good sample of the archaeological sites of the early historic period—perhaps even all of them of village size. Smaller sites do not appear to characterize the settlement hierarchy of the area. I earlier demonstrated (1977) that the area of

Table 4.6. European disease and Coosa River settlement

Coosa River sequence		Documented Florida epidemics (after Dobyns 1983:270, 285)	
Site	Estimated date	Date	Disease
King	1540–70[a]	1535–39	Unidentified
		1564–70	Unidentified and syphilis
Ce308	1570–90		
		1585–86	Unidentified
Terrapin Creek	1590–1600		
		1596	Measles
Bradford Ferry	1600–1630	1613–17	Bubonic plague
Cooper Farm	1630–70	1649	Yellow fever
		1653	Smallpox
		1672	Influenza
Woods Island	1670–1700	1686	Unidentified (typhus?)
		1716	Unidentified

a. Luna apparently found natives in the same location as Desoto, so movement after 1560 is suggested.

the Upper Coosa drainage in the present state of Georgia appears to have been totally abandoned during the sixteenth century (Periods A and B). Since that time, more data have been collected, but the conclusion remains much the same. Figure 4.2 presents data on changes in settlement for the Coosa River area north of the present Childersburg, Alabama. It is believed to be the area of the sixteenth-century province of Coosa known from the de Soto narratives (DePratter et al. 1985; Hudson et al. 1985).

With the exception of the Ogeltree Island site, all sites demonstrably within Period A are located along the upper reaches of the Coosa River drainage system in present Georgia.

Sites that fall within Period B are all downstream in present Alabama; no sites of Period B are known from northwestern Georgia (with the possible exception of the Little Egypt site), suggesting that the area was abandoned before the seventeenth century and not subsequently occupied until much later. In a concentration of sites of Periods B and C in the Weiss Reservoir area of Cherokee County, Alabama, excavations show that the sites did not have late prehistoric components but had relatively short occupations during the early historic period (DeJarnette et al. 1973; Smith 1977). There is another concentration of Periods B and C sites along creek drainages in Talladega County, Alabama, south of Ogeltree Island. This area is probably the province of Talisi mentioned in the de Soto narratives (Hudson et al. 1985). Several Period D sites are known from the Gadsden, Alabama, area, such as the Cooper Farm site. Finally, the Woods Island site (around 1670–1700) is located slightly farther south of the Gadsden cluster.

These distributional data indicate the gradual movement of a cluster of sites (the Coosa Province) down the Coosa River Valley. If we consider Ogeltree Island and sites southward as a separate cluster (the province of Talisi), then we have seven Period A sites in Georgia, two Period B sites in northeastern Alabama, four Period C sites in Alabama (probably only three of which are contemporary—the Terrapin Creek site was probably abandoned early in Period C), and two Period D sites farther south, with the post–early historic period Woods Island site located still farther south. The eighteenth-century location of the town of Coosa is the Childersburg site (DeJarnette and Hansen 1960) located still farther south. The sixteenth-century site of the main town of Coosa is believed to be the Little Egypt site (DePratter et al. 1985; Hudson et al. 1985), the site farthest north. It thus appears that the core of the chiefdom of Coosa shrank from a minimum of five towns to one or two towns and constantly moved southward during the period 1540–1740.

Dobyns has suggested (1983:313–27) that major European epidemics may have been responsible for settlement shifts among aboriginal populations. He illustrates his suggestion by comparing a sequence of historic Seneca Iroquois sites developed from archaeological seriation by Charles Wray and Harry Schoff (1953) with a list of documented and probable epidemics that he has found through analysis of historical records. There is a strong correlation between the archaeologists' estimated dates of occupation and the known occurrences of epidemic disease, suggesting to Dobyns that sites were abandoned because of specific epidemics. How do the epidemics documented by Dobyns match the occupation dates of archaeological sites in our study area?

To test the hypothesis that epidemics resulted in the abandonment of certain sites known archaeologically, the tightly clustered sites on the Coosa River drainage near the present Georgia-Alabama border have been chosen to compare with the epidemics in Florida documented by Dobyns (1983:270, 285). Since he strongly argues that most of these were pandemics, it does not seem unreasonable to compare the interior sites to the Florida epidemics. Table 4.6 compares the site sequence presented in chapter 3 with documented epidemics.

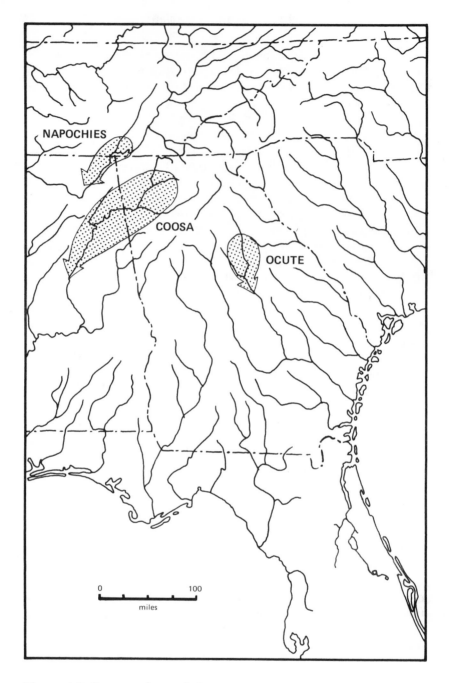

Figure 4.2. Suggested population movements.

(Dobyns also lists possible epidemics, but this application considers only those definitely documented.)

Just as Dobyns found with the Seneca, there appears to be a high correspondence between some settlement shifts and specific occurrences of epidemic disease. The King site, known to have had short occupation (suggested at 1540–70), and perhaps identified in the de Soto (1540) and Luna (1560) documents as the town of Piachi (Hudson et al. 1985), is such a case. Dobyns documents an epidemic of unknown disease during the period 1535–39, just before de Soto, the same epidemic that hit the province of Cofitachiqui in South Carolina. It appears highly likely that the King site was founded just after this epidemic but before the appearance of de Soto in 1540. Similarly, another epidemic of unknown disease of 1564–70 suggested by Dobyns may account for the abandonment of the site and perhaps for the occupation at site 1Ce308 to the south. Again, a documented epidemic of 1585–86 closely matches the estimate of 1590 suggested for the end of the occupation at 1Ce308 and the beginning of the historic component at the Terrapin Creek site, some eleven miles downstream. A 1596 measles epidemic may account for the abandonment of Terrapin Creek and the subsequent movement to the Bradford Ferry site, again closely matching the estimate of 1600.

No documented epidemic closely matches the 1630 estimate for the end of the occupation at Bradford Ferry. Dobyns does list an occurrence of plague in New Mexico in 1630 and a measles outbreak in New England in 1633 (1983:315), but he has no documented evidence of these diseases in Florida. The archaeological evidence, however, suggests that there was a further southward population shift on the Coosa River at this time to the Cooper Farm site. Finally, the estimated abandonment of the Cooper Farm site around 1670 is closely matched by a documented influenza outbreak in 1672.

There seems to have been a high correspondence between diseases and settlement shift in the Coosa area. Only the abandonment of the Bradford Ferry site has not been correlated with a documented epidemic. Obviously the Coosa River area requires further study. Analysis of large skeletal populations might add to the archaeological and historical evidence for settlement shift due to disease. It should also be noted that Dobyns does document other epidemics that do not correlate with Coosa River settlement shifts, so clearly there were factors in addition to disease that caused population shifts.

Population movement can be seen in the Oconee River drainage (fig. 4.2). During the precontact part of the sixteenth century, a powerful chiefdom consisting of three multiple mound sites, two single mound sites, and numerous smaller sites, occupied the Oconee Valley for some sixty miles north to south (Smith and Kowalewski 1980). This is the archaeological Dyar phase and the historically known province of Ocute (Smith 1981) mentioned in the de Soto narratives.

The subsequent Bell phase began about 1600 and lasted until around 1675. European trade material recovered from two sites in the Wallace Reservoir, located approximately in the center of the province, places them in Period C. Several additional sites have produced nondiagnostic European goods. Bell phase sites are small villages or smaller special-purpose sites, and none has mounds (Williams 1983:54).

While downstream movement cannot be clearly demonstrated for the Oconee drainage from the available data, it is apparent that the large mound centers were abandoned. No European artifacts were recovered from relatively extensive excavations at the Dyar mound site, nor were any ceramics characteristic of the Bell phase (Smith 1981). Recent test excavations at the Scull Shoals mound group (Williams 1984; personal communication) recovered one spherical navy blue bead, a type that was in use from Period A through Period D. Some historic occupation is noted for Scull Shoals, but the scarcity of Bell phase ceramics (Williams 1984) argues that the occupation was probably terminated by 1600.

The only known eighteenth-century site on the Oconee drainage is the Oconee Old Town site located near the fall line near Milledgeville, Georgia. Research was carried out at this site by A. R. Kelly with a W.P.A. crew. To date, no report has been made of the findings, but the collections are stored at the Southeastern Archaeological Center in Tallahassee, Florida. This material has been inspected by Mark Williams, who reports that the ceramics are not like the Bell phase material but consist of brushed types typical of those from the Ocmulgee and Chattahoochee drainages (Williams 1983 and personal communication).

John Swanton (1922:179–81; 1946:165) has described the known history of the Oconee. In 1602 the Timucua missionary Pareja mentions that the Ocony were three days' journey from San Pedro (Cumberland Island). In a letter dated April 8, 1608, Ibarra says that the chief of Oconee was marching against the province of Tama. Swanton states that this reference could refer to either of two Oconee groups: one in Florida or one on the Oconee River in Georgia. It is probably a reference to the latter, as the Tama of interior Georgia are no doubt the Altamaha of the de Soto narratives (Swanton 1946:208). Other references to the Oconee noted by Swanton include a 1655 reference to a mission station called Santiago de Ocone, which Swanton places near Jekyll Island, relatively close to the mouth of the Oconee River–Altamaha River drainage system. Ambiguity arises from the fact that there was also an Oconee mission among the Apalachee Indians of Florida in 1680 and from Swanton's interpretations that it had been there as early as 1655. There are references to Oconee Old Town near Milledgeville around the turn of the eighteenth century. Their later movements into Florida do not concern us here.

Swanton's interpretations of Oconee movements are as follows: they were probably on the Chattahoochee River until 1695, when they moved over to the Oconee Old Town Site on the Oconee River near Milledgeville, Georgia. After the Yamassee War, they moved back to the Chattahoochee (Swanton 1946:165).

Another interpretation is offered here. There are references to the province of Ocute in 1540 and 1596 in which Altamaha or Tama are connected. In the 1602 and 1608 references noted by Swanton, the Oconee are also closely tied to the Tama. I suggest that the sixteenth-century province of Ocute became known as Oconee during the seventeenth century. An early English reference (1690) to Chief Altamaha, a powerful Yamassee head man (Wright 1981:158), suggests that the earlier Spanish province of Altamaha became the Yamasee of the English. From this viewpoint, there was population continuity along the piedmont Oconee drainage between the de Soto expedition and the Yamassee War. The Oconee drainage was heavily populated during the sixteenth century (Dyar phase), but its population declined during the seventeenth century (Bell phase). It seems more prudent to show continuity between the groups.

What is suggested, in short, is that because of European-introduced disease, the huge province of Ocute, with its allied town of Altamaha described in the de Soto narratives, shrank into one town, Oconee Old Town, by about 1700. While Williams (1983:440) has correctly pointed out an apparent ceramic discontinuity, an alternative explanation of that phenomenon will be offered in chapter 7. The location of Oconee Old Town at the fall line ecotone and adjacent to the Lower Creek trading path (Goff 1953), which led to Charles Towne, was no accident.

The Tennessee River drainage system settlement distribution is far more complex. It is perhaps most profitably looked at in small segments (figs. 3.1).

The area around Chattanooga, Tennessee, is identified with the Napochies of the Luna narratives of 1560 (DePratter et al. 1985). Current archaeological and historical evidence suggests the following interpretation of population movements. Of sites producing European trade goods, both Citico and Audubon Acres were occupied during the sixteenth century. Audubon Acres appears to have Period A material only, while Citico has at least some Period B material (a few blue beads) and iron chisels that could date to Period A, B, or even C. The overall scarcity of trade goods, and the nature of what there is, suggests placing Citico in Period A to early B. The Citico site is a major mound center; it has produced Southern Cult material (Hatch 1976). The Audubon Acres site is a village (Evans et al. 1981) located up South Chickamauga Creek. It is likely that the sites are contemporaneous, although Citico undoubtedly had a longer occupation. According to the Luna narratives, the first Napochie village was located two leagues from the great river, and another was located on the banks of the river itself. These Napochie villages have been identified with the Audubon Acres and Citico sites (DePratter et al. 1985). Current archaeological evidence, admittedly weak, suggests that Audubon Acres was abandoned before Citico. This view makes sense if European epidemics struck the Napochies and they fell back to their old capital of Citico. The Citico site itself was probably abandoned by 1600. Two Period C sites (1600–1630) are known from this area and no doubt represent later villages of the Napochies. These are Williams Island and Hampton Place (Smith 1976). While these sites may be contemporaneous, the wider variety of trade material at Hampton Place suggests that it is the most recent site in the area, but it does not appear to contain a distinctive assemblage of type D. What happened to the Napochies after 1630? They probably migrated downstream to the big bend of the Tennessee River in Alabama, settling at the Period D sites 1Ms32 and 1Ms91 and finally 1Ms100 late in the seventeenth century (fig. 3.1).

The situation in the Hiwassee River drainage is not as clear. There are two Period A sites, Rymer and Ledford Island, in the middle reaches of the river and a component from Period D on Hiwassee Island at the mouth of the river. Sites of the intermediate Periods B and C are unknown for that drainage, the closest being DeArmond (B) and Upper Hampton Place (B) located on the Tennessee River to the northeast. Data to tie all these sites into one sociopolitical group are not available at this time. The suggested population movement based on dating of sites with European goods is from the Hiwassee River northward to the Tennessee River and then downstream to Hiwassee Island at the junction of the Tennessee and Hiwassee rivers (fig. 3.1). Subsequent early eighteenth-century components are known from upstream in the Hiwassee River drainage, so there was apparently an upstream movement near the turn of the century. These hypothesized movements require further archaeological demonstration. The sites must be shown to be closely related in aboriginal culture.

The Little Tennessee River drainage also presents a complex situation. The Great Tellico site, located up the Tellico River, apparently was occupied from the prehistoric period through Periods A, B, and C. It was also an important eighteenth-century Cherokee site. Although it is known only from surface collections and amateur excavations, the considerable amount of information on Great Tellico available suggests that it was occupied continuously from the early sixteenth through the late eighteenth centuries.

Along the Little Tennessee River proper, there is a great concentration of sixteenth-century European trade goods (Period A) on four sites (Brain 1975; Smith 1976; Polhemus 1982). The mound centers Toqua, Citico, and McMurry were abandoned apparently at this early period, also probably because of disease. No sites with a definite Period B component are recognized in the archaeological record (although Citico may have been occupied), but again there is a cluster of Period B sites located to the northeast on the Tennessee–French Broad river drainage. While at first glance this distribution suggests a movement from the Little Tennessee River to the larger river paralleling the hypothesized movement from the Hiwassee, it should be noted that all three sites (Stratton, Brakebill, and McMahon) have mounds and at least some have long-term occupations in the prehistoric period (especially McMahon, which had a long, documented shell gorget sequence [see Kneberg 1959]). The prehistoric occupation suggests that these sites were not newly settled during the early historic period unless it was a reoccupation of an old town site.

Period C components do occur on sites on the Little Tennessee River proper, including Bussell Island, Tomotley, and perhaps Tallassee. This last site continued to be occupied into Period D. It is thus possible that the Little Tennessee was abandoned during Period B, or right after the Spanish *entradas* of the sixteenth century. The four sites with Period A components are reduced to three sites of Period C and three sites of Period D, again suggesting population decline; however, it is possible that a sampling bias was introduced by only using sites that have produced European goods. The sudden florescence of period D trade goods at sites such as Toqua, Citico, and Tallassee may reflect the entrance of the Cherokee into the Little Tennessee Valley. Specific data indicating European disease in the area have been discussed above in conjunction with the Toqua site.

Some data have been collected on historic occupations on the Clinch, Holston, and Nolichucky rivers (see fig. 3.1), but they do not allow discussions of population movements. The cluster of sites on the Nolichucky River may represent the Chiscas of the de Soto narratives (DePratter et al. 1983).

DePratter et al. (1983, 1985) have identified the Chiaha of the de Soto and Pardo relations with the archaeological site of Zimmerman's Island. Limited archaeological research was conducted on this site before it was inundated by reservoir construction. No European artifacts were found, but aboriginal materials, especially shell gorgets demonstrating a sixteenth-century occupation, were recovered (Kneberg 1959). While we do not have the archaeological data necessary to document the timing of the demise of this Chiaha site, it is interesting to note that they had settled among the Lower Creeks on the Ocmulgee River by 1713, and in 1715 they moved to the Chattahoochee River with the Creek towns (Swanton 1946:115–16). While we cannot prove that there were not two different groups with the same name, it appears likely that the Chiaha fled northern Tennessee sometime in the seventeenth century, possibly to escape other Indian groups armed with firearms from Virginia or the Great Lakes area.

Discussion

Archaeological evidence for depopulation in the study area is not particularly strong. Both mass and multiple burials from the early historic period have been found, but we cannot demonstrate that they were not also present in the prehistoric period. Unfortunately, most of the Period A and many of the Period B sites in the study area also have prehistoric components, and it is thus impossible to contrast clearly protohistoric sites with early historic sites. Indeed, they are frequently the same site, and it is impossible to assign all burials to one component or the other. It can be suggested that mass and multiple burials indicate the occurrence of epidemics, but it cannot be proved at this time.

Evidence from population curves might be suggestive; but to date such analysis has been carried out only on the King site skeletal series, and results from the several analyses are conflicting. It must be conceded that population curves suggestive of epidemics could be the result of famine or other causes.

Indirect measures of depopulation have proven only slightly more useful. There does seem to have been a trend during the early historic period toward a decrease in site size, but data are available for only a few sites. A larger sample of site sizes is needed. While it can be argued that most sites of the early historic period from the Tennessee and Coosa drainages are known, a more intensive survey would generate more confidence in the assertion. The locating of additional sites might severely alter the argument presented here.

Population movements can be documented within the study area, and historical evidence suggests such movements may result from reactions to epidemics. But certainly other events may account for population displacements, among them ecological disasters or warfare.

Carmack and Weeks (1981) point out that archaeological and ethnohistorical data often conflict. While we accept the view of Dobyns and Ramenofsky that southeastern Indian societies underwent drastic depopulation following the introduction of European diseases, the archaeological evidence of epidemics that can be assembled at this time is admittedly weak. But the political breakdown that resulted from this depopulation can be more fully documented. This breakdown of the political structure of the aboriginal Southeast is the subject of chapter 5.

5

The Fall of Chiefdoms

THERE is little doubt that the once powerful chiefdoms in the interior Southeast described by the de Soto narrators were reduced to the small societies that banded together to form the Creek Confederacy by the early eighteenth century. Service (1962:154) has noted that such a change was a common consequence of the influence of foreign civilizations on chiefdoms. He states, "depopulation, defeat, and dislocation, if they are severe enough, reduce the chiefdom to its tribal-like constituent parts or even to the band level or outright extinction. These were consequences most saliently recorded in the history of the Circum-Caribbean chiefdoms after the coming of the Spaniards to the New World (Steward 1948) and for refuge-area Turkic groups in Central Asia."

It is doubtful that anyone would argue that such a process was not acting on the sixteenth-century chiefdoms of the study area. Historical sources from the sixteenth and eighteenth centuries describe contrasting political organizations (see discussion below). But what remains to be done is to demonstrate the process of their transformation archaeologically, to devise means of measuring the process of political change that will have applicability to other areas. The archaeological correlates of chiefdoms proposed by Peebles and Kus (1977) will be used in this study of the disappearance of this political unit from the southeastern United States. Finally, if we use an archaeological approach, what can we say about the timing of the changes from chiefdom societies to less organized groups and confederacies?

Historical background

It is necessary to look first at the historical sources. There is no doubt that the narrators of the de Soto expedition described powerful chiefdoms in the study area. The town of Ichisi is described by Ranjel as having a mound, and Elvas mentions the mound at Tascaluça. Large mounds, of course, imply a centralized power able to direct large groups of laborers. The chief of Ocute sent two thousand Indians to take presents to de Soto and later gave de Soto four hundred carriers (Elvas in Smith 1968:55–56). At several points, towns are mentioned that were subject to a chief; there also were hierarchies of sites under the command of a central chief. Tribute was paid to chiefs; Camuno, chief of Altamaha, asked de Soto if he should continue to pay tribute to Ocute (Ranjel in Bourne 1922:90). Sumptuary laws were clearly in effect: when he came to receive de Soto, the chief of Coosa was carried on a litter borne on the shoulders of sixty or seventy of his principal subjects (Ranjel), and Tascaluca, seated on a cushion on a mound and wearing a feather mantle and a fancy headdress (Ranjel), was attended by many people, one of whom shaded him with a fan of plumes (Biedma). Control of stored food surplus is mentioned; for example, the cacique of Chiaha had twenty barbacoas of maize ready for de Soto (Elvas in Smith 1968:69). These powerful chiefs had advance knowledge of de Soto, and they frequently sent messengers out to de Soto as he entered a chief's territory. Finally, Tascaluca commanded a powerful army at Mabila. All in all, we have a picture of a centralized form of government at the 1540 dateline.

The later Luna and Pardo documents suggest the presence of powerful chiefs, but there are hints that the situation was deteriorating. Luna was asked by the chief of Coosa to aid in a war with the Napochies, who were no longer paying tribute. It is clear from the Luna expedition's accounts that Coosa has lost much of its former glory; the failure to command tribute from the Napochies may be one manifestation of its decline. Nonetheless, with the assistance of the Spaniards, the Napochies were brought back in line (Priestley 1928).

As late as the 1568 expedition of Juan Pardo, highly centralized chiefdoms still existed in the Southeast in the study area. Pardo cemented political alliances by giving gifts to chiefs, "commanders" (war chiefs?), and "principal men" (DePratter and Smith 1980:70). In the Bandera account of the second Pardo expedition, mention is made of hierarchies of chiefs, the use of a sumptuary litter, and chiefs who controlled large quantities of grain. Little seemed to have changed (Bandera 1569).

Seventeenth-century accounts of the study area are virtually non-existent. The available references discuss Ocute/Oconee and Tama. The Spaniards' journey to Tama and Ocute in 1596 was discussed earlier; it gives no good information on the state of affairs in the Georgia piedmont. However, in 1608, Governor Ibarra mentions that the chief of Oconee was marching on the province of Tama (Swanton 1922:179), suggesting that the previous tribute-paying status of Altamaha to Ocute had been disrupted, much as the Napochies had revolted from tribute to Coosa in the 1560s. This disruption probably indicates a deterioration of the earlier political organization.

By the time eighteenth-century documents give us a good picture of groups in the study area, the Creek Confederacy had appeared and the ancient, powerful chiefs had been replaced by mikos. Swanton states, "Theoretically, the miko was little more than the head of the tribal council and spokesman of his tribe, but his actual power varied with his individual ability" (1928:279). Furthermore, the miko acted only after conferring with his council. The miko was normally chosen from a particular clan, and it is suggested here that this practice was probably a vestige of the chiefly conical clan organization. Nonetheless, the position of miko was not hereditary like the earlier position of chief; the miko was chosen by a group or council, whose membership varied among different Creek towns, and he could be replaced or could resign on his own (Swanton 1928:281).

The miko governed a town, or talwa. Swanton equates the term *talwa* with "tribe" in its usual sense. "Some bodies which the Creeks called talwa were once independent, and anciently it is probable that the term applied only to distinct tribes and that in later years it was used for those same tribes as constituent parts of the Creek Confederation" (Swanton 1928:276). In more modern terminology, it seems certain that Creek talwas may have been the remnants of the once powerful chiefdoms. Where complex chiefdoms had existed—that is, chiefdoms built up of a hierarchy of towns (Steponaitis 1978), usually called provinces in the parlance of the sixteenth-century Spaniards—the notion of talwa is perhaps best equated with major towns of the province rather than the province itself. A province or complex chiefdom of the sixteenth century probably "devolved" into several Creek talwas by the eighteenth century. We can demonstrate that a change took place from highly organized chiefdoms, some of which were complex chiefdoms in Steponaitis's terminology, to a confederation of individual tribal groups or talwas, each led by a miko and town council. What are the archaeological correlates of this process of disintegration, and can we determine when the change took place?

Before proceeding, it must be noted that the fall of the chiefdoms was closely tied to depopulation from disease and famine and the loss of culture that ensued. It seems certain that the loss of manpower had much to do with the changes in political organization.

Archaeological correlates

Several factors in the demise of chiefdoms will be considered here; the end of public works such as mounds and palisades; the loss of a settlement hierarchy or at least its simplification; the breakdown of status systems as reflected in grave goods; and the breakdown in organized, part-time craft specialization. These are precisely the correlates of ranked societies (chiefdoms) proposed by Peebles and Kus (1977: 431–32).

Public works

Mound building was an important activity among the protohistoric groups of the study area. The numerous temple mounds found there served as platforms for chiefly residences and mortuary temples. The mounds attest the coercive power of the chiefs to conscript labor for large-scale construction. Some are large: mound A at Etowah (Itaba) is approximately 60 feet high; Shinholser mound A (Altamaha) is approximately 17 feet; Shoulderbone mound A (Ocute) is approximately 35 feet high; and many others were over 20 feet. Still, it must be remembered that they were built in stages over hundreds of years, indicating the long-term stability of the chiefdoms. Although some chiefdoms rose and fell and territories contracted and expanded (DePratter 1983), the archaeological evidence of long-term occupations for many sites indicates that the chiefdoms in the study area were relatively stable. Table 5.1 presents estimates of the occupations of some of the major mound sites in this area. Some appear to have been occupied for as long as five hundred years; thus the cessation of mound building seems to reflect the political, social, and demographic collapse brought about by European contact.

Table 5.2 presents data on mound construction for the sites in the study area. Unfortunately the archaeological data are not as complete as could be wished. Almost all mound sites with European artifacts characteristic of Period A can be shown to have had prehistoric com-

Table 5.1. Mound occupation span

Site name	Historic name	Height of largest mound (in feet)	Ceramic complex	Estimated date	Reference
Abercrombie	—	15	Lamar-Ocmulgee Fields	1565–1685	DeJarnette 1975:154
Brakebill	Chalahume	20	Dallas	1400–1600	Willey et al. 1978:165
Citico 40Ha65	Napochies	25–27	Dallas	1250–1600	Hatch 1976:95
Dyar	Cofaqui	35	Etowah–late Lamar	1000–1550	Smith 1981
Etowah	Itaba	60	Etowah-Lamar	1000–1560	Wauchope 1966:251–59
Lamar	Ichisi	24	Early and late Lamar	1400–1550	Smith 1973
Little Egypt	Coosa	12+	Little Egypt and Barnett Phase Lamar	1400–1600	Hally 1980
Scull Shoals	Patofa	35	Savannah–late Lamar	1000–1600	Williams 1984
Shinholser	Altamaha	25	Savannah-Lamar	—	Wauchope 1966:430; Mark Williams, pers. comm.
Shoulderbone	Ocute	35	Savannah-Lamar	—	Georgia site files; Mark Williams, pers. comm.
Toqua	—	24	Dallas	1215–1620[a]	Richard Polhemus, pers. comm.
Wilson	—	20	?	?	Moore 1915:335

a. Based on radiocarbon determinations.

Table 5.2. Mound construction

Site	Period	Village burials with European goods	Inclusive mound burials with European goods
Abercrombie	B	•	
Brakebill	B		•
Bussell Island	A, C		•
Charlotte Thompson	A–C		•
Citico 40Ha65	P–B	•	
Citico 40Mr7	P?–A	•	•
Cox	A	•	
DeArmond	P–B	•	
Dyar	P[a]		
Etowah	P–A	•	
Great Tellico	P–C	•	
Little Egypt	P–B		•
McMahan	P–B		•
McMurray	A		•
Scull Shoals	P–B?	Unassociated bead	
Stratton	B		?
Talassee, Tenn.	C–D[b]	•	
Taskigi	P, C	•	
Toqua	P–A	•	
Williams Island	P–C[b]	•	
Wilson	A	•	

NOTE: P = prehistoric component.

a. No European goods excavated; ceramics suggest the site was occupied in the mid-sixteenth century.

b. Not known if mound is contemporaneous with historic village.

ponents. This factor could not be determined with the available evidence for Charlotte Thompson, Bussell Island, McMurray Mound, Wilson, and Cox. Of these, all but Wilson and Cox have burials with European artifacts clearly not intrusive into the mound, according to the excavators, and it is entirely possible that these sites were occupied for the first time during Period A. If the Charlotte Thompson site is indeed the Athahachi of the de Soto chronicles, this fact would fit well with the available documentation. Athahachi was noted by Ranjel to be a new town when de Soto visited (Bourne 1922:120).

Many mound sites listed in table 5.2 have produced European trade material from the village area only, so the precise date of the final stages of mound construction cannot be demonstrated by such material. Analysis is further complicated by the fact that a century of farming and erosion often destroys the terminal mound stages.

Within these limitations, nonetheless, a few statements can be made. Virtually all of the sites with historic burials in the mounds have been assigned to Period A or B based on the artifacts present. Only Charlotte Thompson (definitely) and Bussell Island (possibly) have artifacts located within the mound that have been assigned to Period C. Both of these sites were excavated about the turn of this century (Moore 1915; Thomas 1894), so we can never be certain that some of the materials were not intrusive. Mound construction must have ceased by the end of Period C (1630) since no mound contains Period D material that cannot be shown to be intrusive. Many Period A sites that can be shown to have had short-term occupation (probably founded during Period A) do not have mounds (examples include King, Rymer, Ledford Island). Sites of Period B that contain trade materials in the mounds are known primarily from early excavations. These sites include McMahan, Stratton mound, and Brakebill mound, any or all of which may have been contacted by the Juan Pardo expeditions of the late 1560s. Thus they may have received their European goods early in Period B or very late in Period A. The occupation span of most of these sites is unknown due to lack of excavation. It is possible that the mounds were begun prehistorically.

The data indicate that no new mounds were begun after Period B, perhaps not even after Period A. There is some weak evidence that Charlotte Thompson received some mound construction in Period C; however, no other site shows evidence of mound construction after Period B. Charlotte Thompson definitely has Period C materials in the mound, but they may be intrusive.

Some mound sites have produced historic artifacts only in the village area, so the relation of mound building to village occupation cannot be demonstrated. Occupation after Period B cannot be demonstrated for most of these sites with a few exceptions (table 5.2). The Great Tellico site appears to have been occupied continuously from prehistoric times through Period C and was obviously an important place. It also has a large eighteenth-century component and may have been occupied throughout the seventeenth century. The Period C occupation at Taskigi may represent a reoccupation of a prehistoric mound site inasmuch as the mound was constructed considerably earlier (Vernon Knight, personal communication). Williams Island is a complex site; it may have been occupied continuously. The relation of village-recovered trade goods to the mounds on the island is unknown because the site was looted. The Post Oak Island site is also poorly known (Richard Polhemus, personal communication). At the Tallassee site in Tennessee, Period D artifacts were recovered from a village area downstream from a "prehistoric substructure mound" (Cornett 1976:11). The relation of this mound to the excavated village area is unknown. The mound may be considerably earlier than the historic burials in the village area.

Period D artifacts have been recovered from the villages of the Toqua and Citico sites in the Tellico Reservoir. The extensively investigated Toqua site does not show evidence of Period B or C occupation, and the Period D occupation is considered here a reoccupation by later Cherokee arrivals. The Citico site cannot be dismissed as readily. It is possible that Citico was occupied throughout the early historic period, although the evidence is tenuous. Because the later historic burials all come from the village area, the relationship between village occupation and mound construction is again largely unknown. It is clear that early Spanish trade material was recovered from the mound (Thomas 1894; Brain 1975), which probably dates from Period A. Although Clarksdale bells are found in sites of Periods A–C, their context at Citico, as well as the lack of any other European artifacts in the mound, argues for Period A placement.

While no European artifacts diagnostic of Period A or B have been found in the Wallace Reservoir, it can be shown by radiocarbon determinations and ceramic seriation that mound sites such as Dyar (Smith 1981) were abandoned during the sixteenth century. The two sites that produce Period C European goods in the Wallace Reservoir are small village or hamlet sites with ceramics characteristic of the succeeding Bell phase. Thus we can confidently place cessation of mound building in the Wallace Reservoir area of the Oconee River before 1600.

The nearby Scull Shoals mound, tested in the summer of 1983 by Mark Williams, has produced one blue glass bead from the village area, indicating that the site was occupied during the historic period. (Williams 1984). This bead variety was in use throughout the early historic period. More excavation is needed to document the historic occupation of Scull Shoals, but at this point the evidence from the European bead and from ceramic seriation indicates little, if any, occupation in the seventeenth century.

To summarize, it appears that in the study area no new mounds were begun after 1600 (perhaps even 1570), although a few mounds may have been added to as late as 1630. By Period D, we cannot demonstrate archaeologically that any mound centers were even occupied by the groups that had built them. Thus, if mound construction is taken as a measure of chiefly organization, we can infer that such organization began to deteriorate in the late sixteenth century.

Another possible indicator of the decline of chiefly authority is the end of the construction of another type of public works: defensive palisades and ditches. Just as with mounds, the construction of palisades and ditches shows a tremendous investment of labor. From the de Soto narratives, we learn that fortifications were commonly constructed in the Ridge and Valley province but not in the Piedmont during the sixteenth century. For that reason, we will concentrate on the Ridge and Valley province.

Archaeological identification of fortification systems can often be difficult. Fortification systems with ditches are the easiest to locate because often the ditch will remain visible, even after plowing or silting. Aerial photography often can assist in the identification of fortifying ditches or even palisades, but any such identification is specific to each site. What is obvious on some sites is so totally obscured on others that only through excavation can such features be recognized. Since extensive excavations are rare on most sites and since small excavations are usually conducted nearer the center of the sites, data on the presence or absence of palisades are hard to obtain.

Dating of palisade features on sites of long occupation is difficult. Even after extensive excavations, palisades recognized from ground level or aerial observation often cannot be dated. Therefore, when trying to determine when such fortification systems ceased to be constructed at sites with long occupations, the evidence must be viewed circumspectly.

While it can certainly be demonstrated that groups on the tribal level constructed fortifications, let us continue with the hypothesis that a sudden end to palisade construction signaled a loss of political authority of once powerful chiefs. Table 5.3 presents data on palisades for sites in the study area. Lack of excavation makes it difficult to argue that any other given site was not palisaded, and it will not be attempted in this section (but see below).

At present, we can show the presence of palisades on eight sites in the study area that can be dated with European artifacts. Six of them are Period A, including some sites of brief occupation like the King site, where it is clear that fortifications were constructed during the historic period. The Period B Upper Hampton Place site also has a definite palisade that probably cannot be attributed to an earlier component. Finally, the Period D site, 1Ms91, has a double-wall trench feature, "possibly a palisade" (Webb and Wilder 1951:115), which cre-

Table 5.3. Presence of palisades

Site	Palisade present	Period	Reference
DeArmond	Unknown	—	
Austin Springs	Yes	A	Richard Polhemus, pers. comm.
Etowah	Yes	A	Larson 1972
King	Yes	A	Hally 1975
Ledford Island	Yes	A	McClung Museum field notes
Rymer	Yes	A	McClung Museum field notes
Toqua	Yes	A	Schroedl and Polhemus 1977
Citico 40Mr7	Yes	A–?D	Salo 1969:31
Upper Hampton	Yes	B	McClung Museum field notes
Hampton Place	Said to be present	C	
Tomotley	No	C	Guthe and Bristline 1978
Hiwassee Island	Yes, but prehistoric	D	Lewis and Kneberg 1946
1Ms32	No	D	Webb and Wilder 1951
1Ms91	"Possibly a palisade"	D	Webb and Wilder 1951:115

ates a problem in the analysis; but the feature may not be a palisade, and the site is late enough that some groups having firearms may have threatened it, making extraordinary defensive measure necessary.

While data on the presence or absence of palisades are not always available, an indirect measure may suggest their absence. Most palisaded towns were circular, oval, or square (usually with well-rounded corners), and their houses were usually spaced closely, often around a central courtyard (for example, the King site [Hally 1975]). By the eighteenth century, settlement structures were more dispersed and palisades were not constructed around entire towns, although smaller forts may have been constructed in central areas for emergency protection (for example, the Chickasaw forts [Jennings 1941]). Historian Leitch Wright (1981:81) has discussed this process of decentralization: "In English Virginia, and to a lesser extent in Spanish Florida, a trend developed among the natives of living in a less compact fashion. Villages built during the seventeenth century and later tended to be spread out over 1, 2, or 3 miles and not enclosed by a palisade and the percentage of Indians living in isolated houses increased." Wright believed this change to be due to new warfare patterns—"aborigines grew tired of being trapped behind palisades, then burned to death within or shot as they fled." How do the available archaeological data relate to this change in settlement patterns in the study area? Table 5.4 presents available data on site size and length-to-width ratios. It must be remembered that heavy silting, the natural outcome of flood-

Table 5.4. Site shape data

Site	Size (in feet)	Length:width ratio	Palisade?	Reference
Period A (1525–65)				
Little Egypt	1,200×500	2.40:1		Hally 1980:8
Rymer	700×300	2.33:1	Yes	Lewis n.d.
Etowah	3,000×1,500	2.00:1	Yes	Moorehead 1932:1
Toqua	500×350	1.43:1	Yes	Richard Polhemus, pers. comm.
Ogeltree Island	500×400	1.25:1		Alabama site files
Citico 40Mr7	370×300	1.23:1		Richard Polhemus, pers. comm.
Dyar	590×492	1.20:1		Smith 1981
Brown Farm	650×600	1.08:1		Appendix 1
King	480×460	1.04:1	Yes	Hally 1975:17
Period B (1565–1600)				
Abercrombie	ca. 300×300	1.00:1		DeJarnette 1975:154
DeArmond	900×350	2.57:1		McClung Museum files
Upper Hampton	1,400×340	4.12:1	Yes	McClung Museum files
Period C (1600–1630)				
Bradford Ferry	700×100	7.00:1		Alabama site files
Tomotley	500×270	1.85:1		Guthe and Bristline 1978
Period D (1630–70)				
1Ms32	2,640×100	26.40:1		Webb and Wilder 1951
1Ms100	300×150	2.00:1		Webb and Wilder 1951
After Period D				
Woods Island	900×200	4.50:1		Vernon Knight, pers. comm.

ing compounded by culturally accelerated sedimentation (Trimble 1969), has obscured the size of many sites in the study area.

Table 5.4 shows that Period A sites, several of which are known to have been palisaded, all have a length-to-width ratio of less than 2.5:1, while all sites after Period C except the small 1Ms100 have length-to-width ratios exceeding 2.5:1. These sites do not appear, therefore, to have been palisaded but rather to reflect a dispersed settlement strung out along a river. Many of these sites are quite long, for example, 1Ms32 at 2,640 feet and Woods Island at 900 feet; nevertheless, they are not especially large in occupied area.

Hierarchical settlement systems

Another measure of the fall of chiefdoms is the loss of hierarchical settlement systems. Complex chiefdoms have been identified in the study area from both historical and archaeological sources previously discussed, but these systems were collapsing even during the sixteenth and early seventeenth centuries. Historical evidence comes from the Luna expedition's account of the Napochies who refused to pay tribute to Coosa (1560) and the evidence that Oconee was going to fight its previous vassal Tama (1608).

The loss of hierarchical settlement systems can be demonstrated in the intensively studied Wallace Reservoir area and the surrounding Oconee drainage. This large province has been observed archaeologically (Smith and Kowalewski 1980) and has been identified with the province of Ocute mentioned in the De Soto narratives (Smith 1981; Hudson et al. 1984). The prehistoric site hierarchy consisted of one site with five mounds, two sites with two or three mounds, two sites with one mound, and hundreds of villages, hamlets, and special purpose sites (Rudolph and Blanton 1980; Smith and Kowalewski 1980; Shapiro 1983).

To date, all but one of the mound sites have been investigated archaeologically (in modern times), and none has significant components of the well-defined Bell phase (1600–1675). That is, all were abandoned during the sixteenth century (J. Mark Williams, personal communication). Sites of the seventeenth-century Bell phase do not have mounds (Williams 1983), and all known sites of that phase are small villages or special purpose sites. In the Oconee area, the larger politically integrative sites clearly were no longer operational. Population dispersed into small villages and hamlets.

Sites along the Coosa River drainage follow much the same pattern. It has been demonstrated that by around 1600 mounds were not constructed, and by that date mound centers on the Coosa appear to have been abandoned. Site size has been shown to decrease after 1600, perhaps starting to decline as early as Period A (1540–70). Again the hierarchy of large mound centers, smaller nonmound villages, hamlets, etc., appears to have "devolved" into small villages and possibly hamlets.

The same pattern holds for the Tennessee River drainage. Most of the mound centers ceased to function, suggesting a decline from powerful chiefdoms to less centralized groups.

Mortuary practices

Another index of cultural complexity is reflected in the burial rituals of various southeastern Indian groups. Both Lewis Larson (1971) and James Hatch (1975; Hatch and Willey 1974) have noted that aboriginal groups within the study area symbolized the status of important individuals in their burial rituals. Both locational attributes (mound vs. village) and associational attributes (specific artifact accompaniments) were used to symbolize status in these prehistoric chiefdoms. Artifacts indicating high status have been found with burials of all ages and both sexes, and both Hatch and Larson suggest that the status symbolized by these artifacts was ascribed at birth. Peebles and Kus (1977:431) note that "the test for ranking is not merely the presence of richly accompanied child or infant burials." There must be two clearly defined dimensions of mortuary ritual: the superordinate dimension, which is ordered by symbols and energy expenditure but not by age and sex, and the subordinate dimension, which is ordered by age and sex.

In the prehistoric Dallas culture of Tennessee and northern Georgia (now considered the Barnett phase of the Lamar culture, which included such sites as Little Egypt and King), James Hatch has identified artifacts that symbolize the highest status positions: ceramic bottles, massive columella beads, conch shell vessels, copper headdresses, copper earspools, ceremonial celts, and bone pins. Some artifacts, which appear to be exotic, nonetheless apparently symbolize age or sex status. For example, bifacially chipped flint "blades" apparently signify adult male status while rattlesnake gorgets usually accompany subadult burials (Hatch 1975:133). The apparently high-status artifacts are also characterized by their spatial location in a site; that is, they are confined to mound contexts or adjacent to them. In his analysis of the Etowah burials, Larson discusses copper plates, monolithic axes, stone palettes, and copper celts as symbols of high

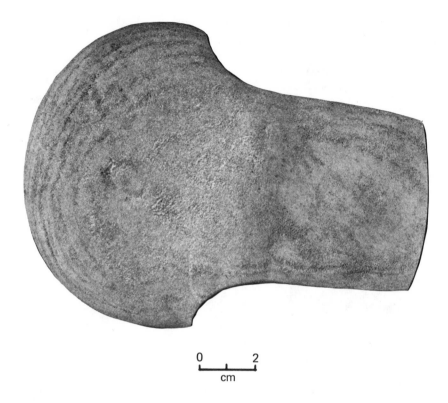

0   2
      cm

Figure 5.1. Spatulate celt, King site, burial 117.

status. Some of these symbols apparently went out of fashion before the early historic period (at least they have not been observed in excavated burials). Some of the other symbols, however, do persist into the early historic period and may be taken as aboriginal markers of high status but not necessarily implying a chiefdom level of organization. To interpret a chiefdom level of organization, the context of these symbols must be analyzed. Currently, there are not enough data for such an analysis; to infer a chiefdom level an archaeologist should be able to demonstrate spatial separation of the chiefly lineage burials and direct evidence of ascribed status rather than only achieved status (cf. Hatch 1975).

Exotic display items that persisted into the early historic period include spatulate stone axes (fig. 5.1) and native copper headdress badges (sometimes used as necklace pendants; fig. 5.2). Both of these

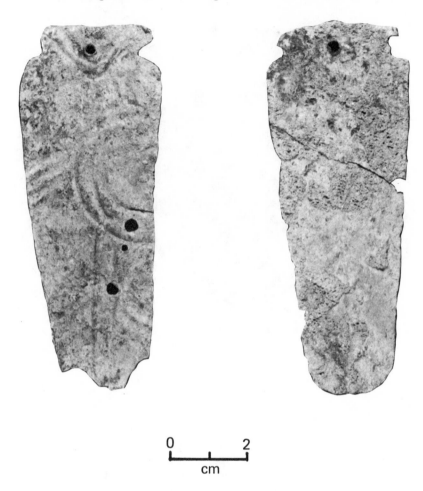

Figure 5.2. Copper badges, King site, burial 92.

are sociotechnic display items and their distribution through time may indicate the demise of the aboriginal status categories. Table 5.5 lists, by period, sites that have produced these status symbols in association with European trade material either directly or just on the site in general (perhaps from earlier occupation of multicomponent sites).

Ground stone spatulate axes were in use for the longest period of time. Such axes have been found in direct burial association with European trade material at the King site and Porch site (Period A), site 1Ce308 and Abercrombie (Period B), Great Tellico (in a probable Period B context), Terrapin Creek (early Period C), and Carter House

(Period C). Thus it is apparent that spatulate axes, which reached popularity as early as the Southern Cult burials at Etowah (Larson 1971:63), probably around A.D. 1350, remained valuable markers of status until the early seventeenth century. Terrapin Creek and Carter House are the only Period C sites that have produced a spatulate axe. It was noted above that the Terrapin Creek site was apparently occupied very early in Period C, abandoned perhaps by 1610. The Carter House site is poorly known and may reflect occupation early in Period C (Polhemus 1982). Sites such as Bradford Ferry and Tomotley with good samples of burials (47 and 92, respectively) have not produced spatulate axes. With the present evidence, we can therefore determine that spatulate axes, as elite sumptuary goods, were no longer used after around 1610. That the idea persisted somewhat longer is shown in the copper or brass spatulate axe recovered from a mid to late seventeenth-century context in Alabama (Greer 1966; see also the Tuckabatchee plates described by James Adair in the eighteenth century [1930:188].

The evidence for the use of native copper is not as clear (table 5.5). Ten of the sites produced native copper, but only at the King site (Period A) and Abercrombie site (Period B) has it been found in direct association with European artifacts (fig. 5.4). Here the native copper artifacts were arrowhead-shaped pendants of the type found used as headdress elements in mound C burials at Etowah (Larson 1959). However, at the King site, these ornaments were used as elements in a necklace of shell beads. This use might suggest that these were heirloomed items reused in a new context. Moore (1900:332) reports similar objects from the Charlotte Thompson Place, but it is not clear from the published report that the native copper was associated with European artifacts. It is possible that the native copper items from all other sites were in prehistoric components. The latest site with native copper is the Terrapin Creek site (late Period B or early Period C), which also has produced the arrowhead-shaped pendants but not in direct association with European goods. Since all data from the Terrapin Creek site have been derived from collectors, the length of occupation of Terrapin Creek is unknown; it may have a prehistoric component. With the available data, we can again estimate that the use of embossed native copper ornaments, believed to symbolize the chiefly lineage, is almost entirely limited to the sixteenth century.

The implication drawn from the study of the distribution of native copper and spatulate axes, already demonstrated to be markers of the chiefly lineage prehistorically, is that the sumptuary goods symbolic of chiefly power were no longer being used by the early seventeenth cen-

Table 5.5. Presence of aboriginal status markers

Site	Spatulate axe	Associated with European item?	Embossed native copper	Associated with European item?	Reference
Period A (1525–65)					
Charlotte Thompson	●		●	?	Moore 1900
Citico 40Ha65	●		●		Hatch 1976; Moore 1915
Citico 40Mr7	●		●		Richard Polhemus, pers. comm.
Brown Farm	●				S. L. Hunter, pers. comm.
Cox	●				Webb 1938
Etowah	●		●		Larson 1971; Moorehead 1932
King	●	●	●	●	University of Georgia files
Ledford Island	●		No		McClung Museum files
Porch Farm	●	●	No		Langford and Smith 1986
Rymer	No		No		McClung Museum files
Toqua	●		●		Richard Polhemus, pers. comm.
Period B (1565–1600)					
Abercrombie	●	●	●		Brannon 1930; Frank Schnell, pers. comm.
1Ce308	●	●	●		Little and Curren 1981
DeArmond Village	No		No		McClung Museum files
Great Tellico	●	●			Rice 1977
Terrapin Creek	●	●	●		Hunter collection; Peek collection; Appendix 1
Upper Hampton	No		No		McClung Museum files
Period C (1600–1630)					
Bradford Ferry	No		No		DeJarnette et al. 1973; M. Smith notes
Carter House	●	●			Polhemus 1982
Hampton Place	●				Polhemus 1982; Tennessee Archaeological Society 1982
Tomotley	No		No		Guthe and Bristline 1978

tury and that use had possibly stopped earlier. It is inferred that chiefly power had eroded severely by this time, and the chiefdoms of the sixteenth century were probably well along toward disintegrating into the societies recontacted by Europeans in the late seventeenth century.

Another method for viewing the breakdown in the chiefly prestige system is to consider the frequency of grave goods among the burials. It could be hypothesized that, in a highly ranked chiefdom, access to mortuary goods would be limited to persons of considerable power; in a more egalitarian society, everyone would have equal access to goods and only the ability to achieve status would limit the ability to accumulate items of wealth for later funerary display. It has been suggested already that in the sixteenth century European material was both rare (scarce) and exotic and was probably controlled by the chiefs. If chiefly power eroded and European goods became more plentiful over time, then the frequency of burials with such objects should have increased. Similarly, if highly ranked organization was giving way to a more egalitarian system, then achieved status systems were replacing the importance of ascribed status systems. More burials should therefore contain aboriginal grave goods also.

Table 5.6 presents data on the frequency of grave goods from sites of the early historic period. Sites of Period A have less than 5 percent of the burials accompanied by European grave goods. The King site is the best example. While it could be argued that European items were simply scarce in Period A, it should be noted that two of the five burials that contained European goods had multiple examples. These burials were precisely the ones that also contained native copper and a shell dipper (burial 92) (fig. 5.4) and a spatulate axe (burial 117) (fig. 5.3), the proposed high-rank native sumptuary goods. Thus, it is clear that European goods were hoarded by the elite.

In Period B, data are lacking to support a definitive statement. Data from 1Ce308 are limited to burials reported by amateurs, all of which contained grave goods. The Upper Hampton Place burials in Tennessee probably represent a reliable sample, and here we see a slight increase in the percentage having European grave goods. None of the fifty-two village burials excavated at the DeArmond site produced European goods, but DeArmond has a prehistoric component, making interpretation difficult.

In Period C, we begin to see an increase in the frequency of European grave goods. There are no documented European-Indian contacts in the Coosa-Tennessee drainage system in this period, yet Euro-

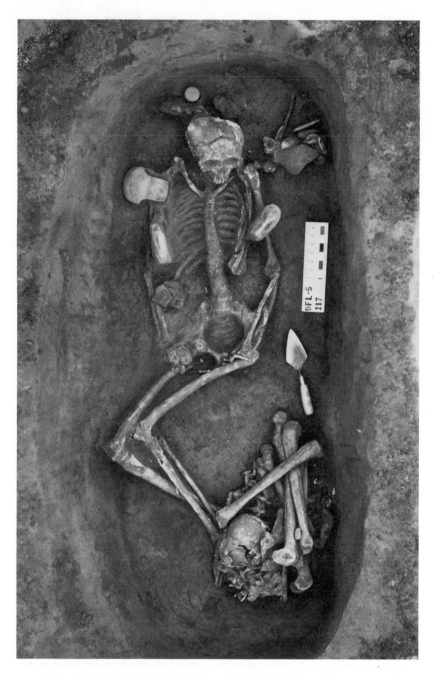

Figure 5.3. Burial with spatulate celt, King site, burial 117.

Figure 5.4. Burial with metal celts, shell dipper, and native copper badges by neck, King site, burial 92.

Table 5.6. Grave goods data

Site	Number of burials	European and aboriginal goods		Aboriginal grave goods	
		Number	%	Number	%
Period A (1525–65)					
Citico	194	4	2.1	76	39.2
King	210	5	2.4	102	48.6
Ledford Island	459	0	.0	134	29.2
Rymer	168	0	.0	39	23.2
Toqua	433	2	.5	104	24.0
Period B (1565–1600)					
1Ce308	14	4	28.6	13	92.9
DeArmond (village)	52	0	.0	19	36.5
Upper Hampton	56	2	3.6	4	7.1
Period C (1600–1630)					
Bradford Ferry	47	13	27.7	18	38.3
1Ce101	17	3	17.6	4	23.5
Hampton Place	31	5	16.1	9	29.0
Tomotley	92	2	2.2	25	27.2
Period D (1630–70)					
Cooper Farm	25	13	52.0	17	68.0
1Ms32	68	9	13.2	16	23.5
1Ms91 (unit 1)	56	5	8.9	10	17.9
1Ms100	73	11	15.1	19	26.0
After Period D					
Woods Island	12	5	41.7	5	41.7

pean grave goods dramatically increase both in frequency and in number. The northernmost site, Tomotley, has only a 5.4 percent occurrence of European grave goods, while the southernmost site, the Bradford Ferry site, has a 66 percent occurrence of European grave goods. These facts suggest that sites farther south were better supplied because they were nearer coastal areas of Spanish influence.

In Period D, the occurrence is similar, ranging from 12.5 to 64 percent. If we average the frequencies for Periods C and D, then an increase in Period D is clearly seen (31.9 to 36.2 percent). But the dramatic shift came after the early historic period. The best evidence is from the Woods Island site (Morrell 1965), which is suggested here to date 1670–1700 and to reflect early English trade out of Charles Towne. At Woods Island, 100 percent of the burials contained European goods.

(Table 5.6)

European grave goods		Burials with grave goods		
Number	%	Number	%	Reference
8	4.1	80	41.2	Richard Polhemus, pers. comm.
5	2.4	102	48.6	Seckinger 1977
0	.0	134	29.2	McClung burial forms
0	.0	39	23.2	McClung burial forms
7	1.6	109	25.2	Richard Polhemus, pers. comm.
5	35.7	14	100.0	Little and Curren 1981
0	.0	19	36.5	McClung burial forms
3	5.4	5	8.9	McClung burial forms
31	66.0	36	76.6	DeJarnette et al. 1973; Smith notes
3	17.6	4	23.5	DeJarnette et al. 1973
12	38.7	16	51.6	Moore 1915
5	5.4	28	30.4	Guthe and Bristline 1978
16	64.0	20	80.0	Lindsey 1964; Battles 1969, 1972; Humbard and Humbard 1965
24	35.3	31	45.6	Webb and Wilder 1951
7	12.5	12	21.4	Webb and Wilder 1951
24	32.9	32	43.8	Webb and Wilder 1951
12	100.0	12	100.0	Morrell 1965

Although the frequency of European artifacts as burial accompaniments increased fairly steadily, the data do not support the hypothesized increase in the frequency of aboriginal materials in burials that was suggested to reflect the change from ascribed to achieved status systems (table 5.6). On most of the sites, 23 to 48 percent of the burials are accompanied by aboriginal grave goods. There is no real discernible pattern in the data except that the sites on the Coosa River generally have a higher frequency of aboriginal grave goods per time unit than the sites on the Tennessee drainage. This fact may reflect the political importance of the core area of the Coosa province. There are a number of possible explanations for the failure of the hypothesis to be confirmed. The increase in European artifacts in burials suggests that these were the desired status markers that were available as the status system changed from ascribed to achieved. Apparently the ancient symbols went out of fashion quickly as the new system and new goods became available. It is also possible that the hypothesis is incorrect.

Perhaps it is illogical to expect a greater number of burials to contain grave goods as the status system changed from ascribed to achieved. Since there are only so many upper-level positions in any system, perhaps a better test would be to see if status markers (European or aboriginal) shift from one social unit to several social units. Unfortunately, because such data are not available for a range of sites, this hypothesized measure cannot be tested at this time.

Craft specialization

Peebles and Kus (1977:432) propose "organized, part-time craft specialization, usually coupled with intersocietal trade" as an archaeological correlate of ranked societies. By extension, the loss of craft specialization or the breakdown of long-distance trade networks should be a measure of the breakdown in ranked social systems, or chiefdoms.

The identification of specialized craft production items is frequently difficult. For example, archaeological evidence from the King and Little Egypt sites suggests that flint knapping activity was carried out in individual households (Hally 1980), yet there are exotic forms that were probably manufactured by specialists (for example, the Duck River cache [Brehm 1981] or long "swords" excavated at Etowah [Moorehead 1932]). Ceramics pose another problem. There is little evidence of ceramic production in the study area, but making ceramics was probably a common household activity. Yet there are specialized ceramic forms that must have been produced, or at least decorated, by craft specialists. The same could be said of ground stone; many people could produce a utilitarian celt, but only specialists manufactured monolithic axes.

One type of artifact was surely a specialized craft production item, certainly manufactured by a limited number of people: the engraved Citico-style rattlesnake gorget of marine shell (Muller 1966; fig. 5.5). This artifact was not considered in the discussion of elite status markers because analysis by Hatch (1975:133) indicated that it was consistently associated with subadults, i.e., it apparently symbolized an age status in Dallas culture (including the present Barnett phase of Lamar culture). Table 5.7 presents data on the presence or absence of Citico-style rattlesnake gorgets in the study area on sites with early historic period European trade materials. These gorgets are rarely found in

Table 5.7. Distribution of Citico-style gorgets

Site	Gorget present	Associated with European goods	Reference
Period A (1525–65)			
Audubon Acres	●		Evans et al. 1981
Citico 40Mr7	●	●	Lewis 1960:96
Brown Farm	●		Smith 1976:33
Cox	●		Kneberg 1959
Etowah	●		Moorehead 1932:65
Johnstone	●		Smith 1976:33
King	●		Smith 1976:33
Ledford Island	●		Kneberg 1959
Little Egypt	●		Hally 1980; Moorehead 1932
Thompson	●		Muller 1966
Charlotte Thompson	No		Moore 1900
Rymer	No		McClung Museum notes
Toqua	No		Richard Polhemus, pers. comm.
Period B (1565–1600)			
Abercrombie	●		Frank Schnell, pers. comm.
Brakebill	●		Willey, Guagliardo, and Bass 1978:150
Citico 40Ha65	●		Moore 1915
DeArmond (village)	●		Kneberg 1959
McMahan	●		Polhemus 1982
Stratton	●		Polhemus 1982
Sylacauga Water Works	●		Steele and Hullender 1960
Terrapin Creek	●		Smith 1976:33
1Ce308	●	●	Little and Curren 1981
Period C (1600–1630)			
Hampton Place	●		Tennessee Archaeological Society 1982
Plum Grove	●		Howard Earnest, pers. comm.
Post Oak Island	●		Polhemus 1982
Tallassee, Tenn.	●		Kneberg 1959
Taskigi	●		Smith 1976:33
Williams Island	●[a]	●	Smith 1976:33
Bradford Ferry	No		DeJarnette et al. 1973; M. Smith notes
Joe Bell	No		
Tomotley	No		Guthe and Bristline 1978
1Ce101	No		DeJarnette et al. 1973
1Ce173	No		DeJarnette et al. 1973
9Ge948	No		

a. Variant.

0 1
cm

Figure 5.5. Citico-style rattlesnake gorget, King site.

direct association with European trade goods. There are several possible explanations for this observed distribution. Many of the gorgets
may be prehistoric. In Period A, European artifacts are restricted to
the elite, and rattlesnake gorgets are not symbols of elite power (as
Hatch has demonstrated). Most Citico-style gorgets that are accompanied by European artifacts are found on sites of Period B or C; but
it should be noted that the one gorget found definitely in association
with Period C glass beads is a unique variant of the style, and its tech-
nical sophistication does not suggest that it is a "degenerate" form (fig.
5.5, 5.6).

While grave lots do not tell us much about the temporal dimen-

0   1
⌊___⌋
cm

Figure 5.6. Williams Island gorget.

sions of the gorgets, associations with specific sites that have also
produced datable European artifacts provide a cruder estimate of the
duration of the style. As shown in table 5.7, ten Period A sites (most of
which also have prehistoric components), nine Period B sites (some of
which have prehistoric components), and six Period C sites produced
Citico-style rattlesnake gorgets; no Period D sites have thus far produced one. Several Period C sites with fairly large samples of burials
have not produced rattlesnake gorgets (such as Bradford Ferry with
47 burials and Tomotley with 92 burials). It thus appears likely that
the gorget went out of style, or was no longer manufactured by craft
specialists supported by the elite of the study area's aboriginal popula-

tions, during the period 1600–1630. It was clearly gone by 1630, as no Period D site has produced one. The interpretation that craft specialists were no longer subsidized to manufacture engraved rattlesnake gorgets is supported by the fact that no other type of engraved gorget took the place of the Citico style. The craft specialty of engraved gorget manufacture, with a history in the area spanning perhaps five hundred years and various styles (Kneberg 1959), ceases abruptly during the early seventeenth century. Organized, part-time craft specialization can thus be shown to have ended at precisely the same time that public works were no longer constructed. The disappearance of native copper sociotechnic display items, described previously, also serves as an example of the loss of specialized craft items.

A breakdown in long-distance trade networks cannot be demonstrated. Just the opposite appears to be true. While there is little historical evidence for Europeans in the interior between 1568 and 1673, there is a constant flow of European trade goods into the study area during this interval. Aboriginal trade networks from coastal areas seem to be the most likely explanation for this influx. There is a possibility that these networks were collapsing, but goods were spread by more long-distance traveling to coastal areas frequented by Europeans. The Helms model (1979) of chiefly trade in Panama may be applicable in the southeastern United States: the chief of Tama visited the coast in 1606, as noted above, but one documented trip is little evidence from which to infer a widespread phenomenon.

Various hypothetical measures of the disintegration of chiefly power following European contact have been suggested in this chapter. The end of the construction of public works, changes in burial programs, and the breakdown in craft specialization have been used to determine when chiefdoms disintegrated into the political organization described by European travelers in the late seventeenth and early eighteenth centuries. All these measures suggest that chiefly power was eroded severely by the beginning of the seventeenth century, perhaps during the last quarter of the sixteenth century.

6

The Question of Acculturation

WHILE it is beyond the scope of this chapter to review all of the literature on acculturation, certain contributions are directly relevant to this study. The question to be considered is whether changes in aboriginal cultures during the early historic period were the result of acculturation between the Europeans and the Indians.

Acculturation has been defined as "culture change that is initiated by the conjunction of two or more autonomous cultural systems. Acculturative change may be the consequence of direct cultural transmission; it may be derived from noncultural causes, such as ecological or demographic modifications induced by an impinging culture; it may be delayed, as with internal adjustments following upon the acceptance of alien traits or patterns; or it may be a reactive adaptation of traditional modes of life" (SSRC 1954). This definition of acculturation is broad; most authors define it as a consequence of direct contact. For example, Alfred Kroeber states, "Acculturation comprises those changes produced in a culture by the influence of another culture which result in an increased similarity of the two" (in Foster 1960:7). George Foster goes so far as to emphasize that acculturation is the product of "continuous and prolonged contact between people of different traditions" (Foster 1960:6). He also distinguishes between formal and informal processes of acculturation. Formal processes are intentionally directed (by governments or missionaries, for example); informal processes are by chance. Foster's idea of acculturation involves a dominant donor culture and a recipient culture. He also uses the term "conquest culture" to describe what he views as an "artificial, standardized, simplified, or ideal" culture consciously designed and

113

created to cope with recognized problems (1960:11–12). Clearly, his view that acculturation results from prolonged contact is much more restrictive than the Social Science Research Council's definition, which would appear to accommodate indirect changes such as those which took place in the interior Southeast in the seventeenth century.

Even Foster's restrictive definition is subject to interpretation. How long is "continuous and prolonged contact"? Do the thirty days de Soto spent at Chiaha or the twenty-five days spent at Coosa (Elvas in Smith 1968) constitute such contact? Probably not in Foster's sense. What about Europeans and Africans from the de Soto expedition who stayed in the province of Coosa (Ranjel in Bourne 1922:113)? It is more likely that the Old World people "went native" than that they changed the Indians' culture. What about the forts that Juan Pardo established in the East Tennessee Valley (DePratter et al. 1983)? The evidence is conflicting; the forts may have fallen almost immediately or may have persisted for years (Gannon 1965b:351–52). Whether an acculturative situation of true "prolonged contact" developed is not known.

If a narrow definition of acculturation proposed by ethnologists such as Foster is accepted, then most researchers would agree that no true acculturation took place in the study area during the early historic period. The broader definition proposed by the Social Science Research Council allows for more indirect interaction, and such interaction, evidenced by trade, was indeed taking place. Archaeologists, on the other hand, have developed their own ways to study acculturation.

Archaeological studies of acculturation can be traced to museum studies of material culture items that showed the influence of foreign elements (in this case, European) on aboriginal items (Quimby and Spoehr 1951). Out of this initial attempt to classify artifacts, John White (1975) developed a model for measuring acculturation that will be discussed below.

Later, the Society for American Archaeology developed a classification system for culture contact situations relevant to this study (Wauchope 1956). This scheme, presented in table 6.1, deals with site unit intrusion (the intrusion of a completely different archaeological culture into an area) and trait unit intrusion (the adoption of a new trait within an area). Obviously this scheme was devised for archaeologists looking at specific archaeological sites or traits. The real issue of acculturation, i.e., the process of change in a cultural system, is never really addressed. Despite its limitations and the fact that it does not

Table 6.1. The Wauchope model of culture contact situations

Situations	Example
A. Site unit intrusion	
A1. Retention of cultural identity with little trait change	Norse-Eskimo, 14th and 15th centuries
A2. Fusion with dominance of the resident culture	Macon Plateau, Tiahuanaco horizon sites in Peru
A3. Fusion with dominance of the intruding culture	Spanish missions in Southeast; Lamoka-Laurentian at Frontenac Island site; Roman sites in Britain; intrusion of Inca culture on Peru coast
A4. Fusion followed by revival of the resident culture	Inca conquest of Ica Valley gives way to Ica revival
B. Trait unit intrusion	
B1. Adoption of the trait unit without modification and without fusion of the introduced trait unit with corresponding elements in the receiving culture	Trade objects—glass beads, shells, obsidian; also includes local imitations
B2. Fusion with dominance of the corresponding part of the receiving culture	Chinese influence in Britain in 18th and 19th centuries; Weeden Island–French Fork incised ceramics
B3. Fusion with dominance of the intruded trait unit in the aspect of culture involved	New burial practice introduced; Southern Cult
B4. Fusion with emergence of the new traits that have no obvious antecedents in the trait units of the receiving culture	Sumerian influences in Egypt lead to crystallization of Dynastic Egyptian culture

SOURCE: Wauchope 1956.

differentiate between diffusion and acculturation, the scheme does have some obvious applicability to the interior Southeast of the early historic period.

The only site unit intrusions to take place during the early historic period are the European forts erected by Juan Pardo in the Carolinas and Tennessee (DePratter et al. 1983). These forts apparently did not last very long, and the resulting contact situation is best categorized under "A1: retention of cultural identity with little trait change." Toward the end of the early historic period, more and more aboriginal population movements took place as discussed above, perhaps result-ing in A2 contact situations.

Trait unit intrusion clearly took place during the early historic pe-riod in the form of European manufactured trade goods. These will be discussed more fully below; it will suffice here to note that they were probably subsumed by the category B1 (table 6.1).

Working with the classification scheme for ethnographic material developed by George Quimby and Alexander Spoehr, John White (1975) developed a classification scheme for archaeological remains on European-Indian contact period sites. His scheme is presented in table 6.2. This scheme classifies new types of introduced artifacts as well as old types modified because of contact. Each numbered cate-gory of the two divisions (New Types and Old Types) shows increasing levels of acculturation from low numbers to high. "By determining the relative proportion of each of these artifact types in a contact situation, the archaeologist may provide himself with a rough indica-tor of the degree of culture change in both material and non-material spheres" (White 1975:159–60). Sites producing abundant artifacts that fit the low-numbered categories thus display little acculturation, and vice versa. Note that White assumes that the acceptance of mate-rial items indicates changes in the nonmaterial (mental) realm.

In an earlier work, I argued that the artifacts found in early his-toric period sites on the Coosa River drainage in Georgia and Ala-bama fall into White's categories A1 and B1 (Smith 1977). Before ex-panding the present discussion to include our larger study area, it is necessary to review additional archaeological studies of acculturation.

Ian Brown (1979a, b) has taken the White model one step farther. He notes that White implies that "historic Indian sites can be ar-ranged according to the degree of acculturation solely on the basis of material modifications" (Brown 1979a:113). Brown points out that the same artifact may have a different function in different cultures and criticizes White's model for failing to consider the function of the artifact. He advocates the use of ethnohistoric documents to deter-mine the function of introduced artifacts before inferring a degree of acculturation from their presence. He points out that some items such as beads, bottle glass, and guns, which merely were substitutive in White's model, actually functioned in a socioreligious context in In-dian cultures in the Lower Mississippi Valley—a context gleaned from ethnohistorical accounts that suggest a different picture of accultura-tion than does White's model. Brown goes on to stress the importance of determining the "role of the transmitters of material culture, the

Table 6.2. The John White model

Category	Description	Example
NEW TYPES		
A1.	New types of artifacts received for which there is a native counterpart	Trade beads; European clothing (in some cases); iron knives; ceramic containers where there is a pottery tradition
A2.	New types of artifacts received where there is *no* native counterpart	Bottles; firearms; skillets
A3.	New types of artifacts made from native materials but copying introduced models	
	a. Where the techniques are introduced along with the new artifact	Pottery making
	b. Where the techniques come from within the recipient group	Where there is a change in the materials of manufacture requiring a new set of techniques
A4.	New types of artifacts where the introduced model is decorated after the native manner	Carved handles; European clothing modified in native manner
A5.	New types of artifacts where the manufacture is local but the maker employs imported materials and techniques	Knives converted from raw iron or a less useful article; clothing made by importing cloth and sewing devices
OLD TYPES		
B1.	Old types of artifacts where there is a substitution of an imported material for a local one	Glass projectile points; porcelain gaming pieces; glass or porcelain scrapers
B2.	Old types of artifacts where there is a substitution of material and technique	Metal projectile points; substitution of metal for traditional bone tools
B3.	Old types of artifacts modified by the introduction of a new element of subject matter	Foreign designs on pottery, basketry, petroglyphs

SOURCE: White 1975.

nature of the contact situation, and the use and value of the transmitted materials to the Indians themselves." He also mentions that the archaeological context of the finds is important in helping to determine their function (Brown 1979a:119).

Another major attempt to measure acculturation through archaeological research is presented by Jeffrey Brain (1979). Like Foster,

Brain views acculturation as one possible process of culture change, a process that requires a dominant culture. He stresses that in determining the degree of acculturation, two major dimensions must be measured archaeologically: the artifacts and their contextual configurations. Brain believes that a rough measure of material culture replacement (acculturation in a simple form) is the proportion of traditional aboriginal to introduced European items (compare to the "Iroquois method" for seriation of sites discussed in chapter 3).

A more accurate measure of culture change can be made by determining what Brain calls the "innovation value" of each artifact. The innovation value is determined for five attributes: material, form, technique of manufacture, technique of use, and function. Each artifact is scored 0 for old and 1 for new attributes. The total is the artifact's innovation value (never more than 4 due to overlapping categories). The higher score indicates the greater degree of culture change. Innovation values are then averaged for all artifact *classes* on the site (not individual artifacts or types). In addition to studying the artifacts themselves, Brain also advocates looking at their "configurations" (1979:272). The configuration is determined by the context and associations of the artifact. He uses the example of a European nail. A nail used in an aboriginal manner as an awl would have a low innovation value of 2, but a concentration of nails in a rectangular pattern, suggesting a European-style house, would have an innovation value of 4. Thus scores assigned depend on the artifacts' configurations as well as their innovation value.

Artifact scores and configuration scores together document archaeologically the degree of culture change in a given situation. Their total then represents a locus on a relative scale of aboriginal to acculturated to assimilated conditions. These points are labeled pristine state (score 0), acculturation (scores 1, 2, and 3), or assimilation (score 4).

Brain's artifact categories in actual use borrow heavily from White (1975). In this case (Tunica treasure) there is regrettably little context (the Tunica treasure was recovered by an amateur without documentation), so it is hard to see how Brain's complete scheme for measuring culture change is made operational. Like Brown, however, Brain stresses the importance of considering the archaeological context to interpret the function of the artifact in question before using that artifact to pinpoint the degree of acculturation.

How then can these techniques for measuring acculturation in the archaeological record be used for the early historic period in the interior Southeast? First it is necessary to define acculturation as used in this study: the process of accepting foreign ideas, concepts, material culture, etc., from another culture. It explicitly includes modifying the first culture (in this case aboriginal) toward that of the second (European). This modification must come from within the receptor culture. Thus, for reasons to be presented in this chapter, that portion of the Social Science Research Council's definition that includes changes due to secondary causes (such as demographic or ecological modifications caused by the impinging culture) is rejected. Clearly, this is an important process in culture change in the study area but one that may be excluded from the label "acculturation." Acculturation, then, is the process by which one culture accepts and integrates elements of a second, donor culture. Eventually if the two cultures become identical—that is, if the receptor culture rejects all its aboriginal elements to accept the elements of the donor culture—it is assimilation that occurs. This is a theoretical point, because in the real world it is doubtful that total assimilation ever has, or ever will, take place. Aboriginal cultures appear always to retain some elements of their core belief system, even though they may wholeheartedly accept elements of foreign material culture and utilize them in the same manner as the donor culture.

How can these archaeological measures of acculturation be applied to data from the interior Southeast in the early historic period? How can the early historic period artifacts found in the study area be fitted into the model proposed by John White? And considering the archaeological context of the introduced goods, as suggested by Brown and Brain, what additional inferences may be made?

Artifacts typical of Period A (1513–65) include glass beads, metal beads, brass bells, axes, chisels, wedges, and miscellaneous military hardware. On the surface, it would appear that glass and metal beads simply substituted for shell beads; brass bells were not unlike aboriginal rattles made from turtle shells or gourds; and metal tools were simply substitutes for stone tools.

What can we learn from the context of the finds? As discussed in chapter 5, all European artifacts were very scarce during Period A. When archaeological provenience data are available, these European artifacts are usually interred in what appear to be elite graves. For example, the five burials with European goods excavated at the King site all had additional aboriginal grave goods, some of which were exotic—including a shell dipper and the only instance of native copper. Based on the context of such items, it is suggested that iron chisels, wedges, and axes were substituted not for useful stone tools but for sociotechnic display weapons such as copper celts or ritual forms of stone axes (Smith 1977). Indeed, burial 117 at the King site contained a sociotechnic spatulate stone axe in association with iron implements (fig. 5.3). While metal tools were probably substitutive (i.e., they fit White's category A1 indicating virtually no culture change), it is important to determine their function in the aboriginal culture based upon their context. Sword blades, occasionally found, probably also had the same symbolic value. Instead of being substitutes for functional weapons, they were probably substitutes for the sociotechnic chipped flint knives.

Small tubular beads of rolled European copper or brass occur rarely on A sites but deserve further discussion. These beads were probably substitutes for exotic shell beads. The question is whether they were manufactured by Europeans or by Indians, and, if by the latter, whether their presence implies new technology and thus a higher level of acculturation (White's category B2). Even assuming that the beads were made by the Indians, the techniques were not new. While aboriginal metalworking had reached a peak earlier, probably during the thirteenth and fourteenth centuries (see, for example, Hamilton et al. 1974), and was definitely on the decline when de Soto explored the Southeast, it is clear from finds at several of the sites dealt with in this study that native copper working was still practiced (unless all the pieces were heirloomed). The argument against heirlooming lies in the large amount of native copper that the de Soto chroniclers reported seeing, for example, in the province of Cofitachiqui (Elvas in Smith 1968:72; Garcilaso in Varner and Varner 1951:311, 317). It appears that we can confidently place tubular metal beads in White's category B1, again implying little acculturation. Thus it appears that, using the White model, there was little acculturation during Period A.

Period B artifacts are virtually the same as those of Period A, with the exception of new glass bead styles. European artifacts appear to be more common, probably reflecting the additional material available from coastal trade following the establishment of St. Augustine, Santa Elena, and the Guale missions and additional European goods traded by the Luna and Pardo expeditions at the close of Period A. Unfortunately, we cannot adequately quantify European material from Period B, since many of the sites producing these materials have not been excavated scientifically.

Nevertheless, a few points can be made. Comparing the European

artifacts recovered by amateurs as grave goods from site 1Ce308 on
the Coosa drainage in Alabama (Little and Curren 1981) with the pro-
fessionally excavated Upper Hampton Place site on the Tennessee
River (notes on file at McClung Museum, University of Tennessee), it
can be suggested that European artifacts were more common in the
southern portion of the study area. At least five burials (of an unknown total "over 35") excavated at 1Ce308 produced European
grave goods, and some had several items; only three of fifty-six burials
at Upper Hampton Place had European objects (usually one per burial), and none of fifty-two village burials at DeArmond (a site of long
prehistoric occupation, however) had European artifacts (field notes,
McClung Museum).

   That European artifacts were becoming more common is demonstrated clearly by the fact that several Period B sites produced European artifacts from general midden areas, while all European artifacts
from Period A sites came from burial contexts. Apparently European
artifacts were beginning to lose some of their value as exotic items,
perhaps marking a shift from elite status markers to everyday items of
adornment or functional tools.

   European artifacts of Period C are much more plentiful and include large quantities of glass beads, iron celts and axes, and a sudden
proliferation of brass items: beads, disc gorgets, conical bangles, bracelets, and bells. Nevertheless, they appear to be largely substitutable,
falling into White's categories A1 and B1, implying little acculturation.
Glass beads completely replaced shell beads, and brass gorgets completely replaced shell gorgets at the Bradford Ferry site in Alabama.
Regarding the White model, however, it should be noted that no new
technology was adopted, nor were European artifact types that had
no aboriginal counterparts adopted. Clearly the aboriginal population was not changing its culture, certainly not changing it to a European form. Acculturation was minimal.

   The assemblage of European artifacts of Period D is more diverse.
Glass beads and brass bells are numerous. Iron celts are still found,
but eyed axe forms had become more common. Indeed there is some
evidence that the Indians converted iron eyed axes into smaller chisel
blades (Fleming and Walthall 1978:31–32). This was accomplished by
sawing and grinding, aboriginal techniques again suggesting no new
technology. The fact that they converted eyed axes to celt blades implies either that metal was scarce and they wanted to extend its use or
that they rejected the European hafting technique and preferred to
use their aboriginal style haft, a choice that suggests little accultura-

tion. The fact that iron axes were beginning to show up in refuse at this time, as well as the fact that some axes are quite worn from heavy use, indicates that they no longer functioned in a purely sociotechnic realm but had been accepted as everyday tools.

New styles of brass ornaments appeared, but again they did not really represent a new technology. Small glass "seed" or embroidery beads, which first appeared in some number in Period C, became more common, suggesting the presence of sewn beadwork. The reported occurrences unfortunately do not usually specify how the beads were found in a burial. If beadwork was simply a substitute for shell beadwork or quillwork, then it would be subsumed under White's category B1 and still would not indicate much culture change.

Perhaps the only European artifacts to occur on Period D sites that indicate some real changes in the aboriginal culture are firearms, which are rare (if present at all on true Period D sites). John White uses firearms as an example of his category A2: "New types of artifacts received when there is no native counterpart." He suggests that the presence of such artifacts "implies a greater degree of culture change since a context must be developed to give the artifact function and meaning" (White 1975:161)—not a simple replacement artifact or a new raw material. Nonetheless, this is only Category 2 out of five and still implies relatively little culture change.

Ian Brown cautions that during the late seventeenth century in the Lower Mississippi Valley, firearms were reportedly kept in the temple. He suggests that they served a religious function (Brown 1979a:117). It is entirely possible that at this early period the Indians were unable to obtain powder or shot, that these firearms were kept in the temple as exotic items symbolic of the esoteric knowledge of the priest-chief (cf. Helms 1979), and that they did not function as hunting or war-related weapons at all.

It may be concluded, then, following the model proposed by John White and even considering the modifications proposed by Ian Brown and Jeffrey Brain, that European goods present on aboriginal sites throughout the early historic period suggest that there was only very limited culture change (acculturation). Although more far-reaching changes were taking place, they cannot be measured using the techniques proposed by White.

Trade goods have been adequately considered, but what about other elements of material culture, specifically, the introduction of European plants and animals? De Soto carried pigs inland and even left some with various Indian groups, including Ichisi and Altamaha in the study area (Swanton 1939:91). After the death of de Soto, Moscoso attempted to take the force overland to Mexico. Failing, he returned to the Mississippi River, where he found that some pigs left with the Indians of Gauchoya had multiplied (Swanton 1939:91). Swanton does not believe that pigs were raised by the natives after the de Soto expedition. He notes that there is only "one doubtful reference" to pigs in the area of de Soto's march when Europeans again ventured inland. He says that swine had rapidly spread over the country by this second wave of European exploration. It does seem very unlikely that the farming and hunting southeastern Indians could be converted to stock raising by the brief de Soto contact. A shift to stock raising would imply a high degree of acculturation, the achievement of which no doubt would have required Foster's "prolonged and continuous contact." It is possible that some of the Spanish pigs multiplied in the wild and were hunted by the Indians, but this would imply virtually no acculturation. The zooarchaeological record remains silent; no pig bones have been found (or recognized) from early historic period sites in the interior Southeast.

On the other hand, there is both archaeological and historical evidence that new species of plants were rapidly accepted among aboriginal groups in the Southeast. While the historical accounts all come from areas that are peripheral to the study area, they seem relevant in light of the archaeological evidence to be presented. The two plants to be considered are the watermelon and the peach.

The peach is a native of China and was brought to Rome during the first two centuries B.C. and to the New World as early as Columbus's second voyage, along with melons (Sheldon 1978:28). In 1521, Ponce de León carried "diverse seeds for planting" to southern Florida (Sauer 1971:35). His colonizing attempt was received with hostility by the local Calusa and the colony was aborted, but it is possible that the Indians obtained seeds at this time. It should be noted that Goggin and Sturtevant (1964) claim that the Calusa were nonagricultural, and if they are correct (a point here considered debatable; see also Dobyns 1983), then it is doubtful that European plants were adopted at this time.

A 1525 voyage to the Atlantic coast sent by Ayllón cruised 250 leagues along the coast, contacted four linguistic groups, and left the seeds of European plants with aboriginal groups in the Santee River area of South Carolina (Hoffman 1980). The Luna colonizing venture on the Gulf coast in 1559–61 undoubtedly carried seeds to the New World; however, most supplies were lost in a bad storm, and it is not known if any seeds were salvaged by colonists or Indians (Priestley 1928).

The French garrisons of the 1560s apparently did not successfully grow much food. They were bartering constantly with the Indians (Bennett 1975), and it is therefore judged unlikely that they introduced Old World plants.

Later when Spanish colonies were established firmly at St. Augustine and Santa Elena and mission efforts began among the Guale in the 1560s, many European plants were introduced. "By the late 1560s, mutual agricultural interchange had taken place between North America and Iberia. Fruits and vegetables from Spain and the Canary Islands—oranges, figs, squash, and other items—had been successfully introduced" (Lyon 1981:288).

It is clear that peach trees were grown at most Spanish-Indian missions in the Southeast, perhaps at all of them. Sheldon (1978:28) notes that the earliest written record of the Spanish introduction of the peach to continental North America is 1602: the Franciscan mission garden at St. Augustine was producing peaches and many other European plants. It should be noted also that Governor Oñate (around 1601) saw watermelons growing in the pueblos of the Southwest.

There is no doubt that European-introduced plants quickly spread throughout North America. In 1663 the English explorer Hilton saw peaches growing in coastal South Carolina (Sheldon 1978:28), as did Henry Woodward some three years later near Port Royal (Wright 1981:105). These were no doubt introduced by Spanish missionaries.

By the late seventeenth century, French explorers found peaches, watermelons, and even chickens among native groups along the Mississippi Valley. In 1682 LaSalle saw abundant peach trees and chickens at the mouth of the Arkansas River; in 1687 both peaches and watermelons were mentioned in the same area, and watermelons were also seen at Fort St. Louis in Illinois. LaSalle had earlier reported watermelon vines among the Cenis of eastern Texas (Sauer 1980:241–42). Sauer believes that these were introduced via the Spanish-occupied Southwest; it is also possible (but less likely) that they came from the Apalachee missions in western Florida. Whatever their origin, the plants had been spread by aboriginal farmers far from their point of introduction.

What about archaeological remains? The only ones are peach pits, which are common finds in seventeenth-century Spanish mission villages in Florida. For example, at Fig Springs, nearly a bushel of peach pits was recovered from the post-1650 Utina site (Deagan 1972:39).

They have also been recovered from the Apalachee mission San Francisco de Oconee (Boyd et al. 1951:124).

Peach pits have also been recovered in St. Augustine in a context of about 1580 (Deagan 1978:135) and from the sixteenth-century town of Santa Elena (Scarry 1983:118). Within the study area, they have been found in the Joe Bell site in the Wallace Reservoir on the Oconee River. This site has corrected radiocarbon date determinations of 1620 and 1630 (Williams 1983) and trade material appropriate to Period C (blue beads). Several other sites in the Wallace Reservoir have produced peach pits. All are assigned to the Bell phase; they include 9Ge958 and 9Mg185 (Ledbetter n.d.) and 9Ge237 (Wallace Mitigation Survey—North Survey Rough Analysis, manuscript on file at the University of Georgia). These peaches may have been brought in by aboriginal traders from the Guale missions near the mouth of the Oconee-Altamaha river system or by the missionaries who visited Ocute in 1596.

Another possible instance of evidence of peaches in the early historic period was recovered at the Citico site 40Mr7 in the Tellico Reservoir in eastern Tennessee (Richard Polhemus, personal communication). Here a burial accompanied by an aboriginal shell gorget with drilled pit decoration was intrusive on a feature that contained peach pits. Gorgets with drilled pit decoration have been recovered from the Period B 1Ce308 site (Little and Curren 1981:130) and from the Period A–C Charlotte Thompson Place (Curren 1983). The Citico burial is placed tentatively in Period B or perhaps Period C. That these eastern Tennessee peaches are potentially as early as those from the Joe Bell site in Georgia suggests the rapid spread of peaches across the interior Southeast.

It is thus apparent from both historical and archaeological sources that European plants spread across the Southeast during the early historic period. Most early excavations (W.P.A. and earlier) did not recover floral remains; therefore, archaeological evidence is scant. More archaeological research needs to be done to determine when peaches reached the interior Southeast. At this point, an early seventeenth-century date can be supported through archaeological evidence. It is possible that peaches spread into the interior Southeast shortly after the founding of St. Augustine, Santa Elena, and the Guale missions in the 1560s. But what does this say about acculturation?

Since the southeastern Indians had been horticulturists for centuries, it is not surprising that they rapidly accepted new plants such as watermelons. Planting melon seeds was just as easy as planting the squashes or corn they grew. Planting peach pits was also just as easily accomplished, but it must be noted that the southeastern Indian did not plant orchards prehistorically. While it might be argued that planting peach trees and waiting several years for a harvest is a quite different type of agriculture than annual cropping, it can also be argued that it is only a difference of degree, not of kind. Peach cultivation is basically a substitutive process analogous to White's example of the substitution of glass beads for shell beads.

To break away from materialistic evidence of acculturation, what about more ideological realms of acculturation? Specifically, what was the impact of Spanish Catholic religious teachings on the Indians of the interior?

Hernando de Soto brought missionaries into the interior as he traversed the Southeast in the 1540s. Crosses were erected at several sites in the study area (Ichisi, Altamaha, and Ocute, for example), and no doubt religious instruction was delivered to the natives. It is unlikely that this brief encounter with Christianity had any real effect on the natives, at least not immediately. If we accept the hypothesis that European disease quickly reduced populations and that Indian religious specialists were dying off faster than their teachings could be passed down (Hudson 1980), it could be hypothesized that the surviving natives would be more willing to accept new teachings. The sudden appearance of the technologically superior Europeans, with their control of horses, might be enough to force the Indians to question their belief systems, which did not explain such things. As coastal Indians began to die of European-introduced disease, they no doubt noted that the Spaniards were less seriously stricken, and this word must have spread quickly into the interior. The Huron in Canada noted the apparent immunity of their Jesuit missionaries to the disease epidemics that ravaged them (Trigger 1976), and they attributed this immunity to witchcraft. It would be unusual if the natives did not have some interest in the religious beliefs of the invaders in these circumstances.

Juan Pardo took missionaries into the interior in 1566–68, and at least one, Sebastian Montero, may have remained in the interior of North Carolina until 1572 (Gannon 1965b). While Montero was far to the east of the study area, the natives may have received some religious instruction from Spaniards at Pardo's other forts, some of which were located in the study area in eastern Tennessee (see DePratter et al. 1983). These forts may have fallen as early as 1568 or may have been occupied as late as 1576 (Gannon 1965b:352). Apparently, the forts did not have resident priests; Montero had been the chaplain of the Pardo expedition, and he elected to continue the expedition, moving out of the study area.

The 1596 expedition of Gaspar de Salas and two Franciscans, Fathers Pedro Fernandez de Chosas and Francisco de Veras, visited Tama and Ocute, but they returned almost immediately when they were warned of hostile Indians. In 1606 the chief of Tama traveled to Sapelo Island to meet with Governor Ibarra (Swanton 1922:181–82). These two documented occurrences of contact suggest that the Indians on the Oconee drainage may have been in close contact with the Spaniards (missionaries) on the coast. Given the hypothesized loss of elements of the aboriginal belief system, it is quite possible that many converts to Christianity were made in this area. Indeed, by 1655, there was an Oconee mission, San Francisco de Apalache, among the Apalachee in western Florida and another, Santiago de Ocone, perhaps on Jekyll Island on the Georgia coast (Swanton 1922:179).

Again, how is this limited evidence to be interpreted when measuring acculturation in the interior Southeast during the early historic period? Apparently, the Indians of the Oconee Valley, at least, had been subjected to, and had probably accepted, Christian training by the first half of the seventeenth century. It is difficult to determine to what extent Christian beliefs were accepted. If the Indians only adopted portions of the Christian religious system to supplement their aboriginal beliefs, then a lesser degree of acculturation is implied than if they accepted Christianity as a replacement for their aboriginal system. The latter extreme seems unlikely. The acceptance of Christianity, however restricted, did represent a fairly high degree of acculturation, certainly more than the replacement of aboriginal shell beads with glass beads. But how did this affect the study area as a whole? The evidence indicates that the study area generally was little affected, as, indeed, perhaps was even the Oconee Valley. Evidently, the Christianized Indians were relocated quickly on the Georgia coast or with the Apalachee in western Florida. Thus, the traditional southeastern Indians were left to live a relatively unacculturated existence in their homeland. There was probably little ideological change toward the European worldview in other areas of the interior Southeast until Europeans again invaded the area and continuous contacts were resumed.

Based on historical evidence and archaeological schemes designed to measure acculturation, it seems clear that little acculturation took place in the study area during the early historic period. Conversely, as argued in chapters 4 and 5, a great deal of culture change did take place. There is a fine line between this culture change and acculturative change, particularly considering the broad definition of acculturation proposed by the Social Science Research Council, but it is an important distinction. The change that took place during the early historic period was basically a loss of culture— "deculturation" is the controversial term used by Julian Steward (Steward and Faron 1959: 176). As demonstrated archaeologically here and by the historical record, populations declined drastically, chiefdoms disintegrated, settlement patterns were disrupted, and, as Charles Hudson argues, probably elements of the belief system were lost. The Indians of the interior were likely left in a sort of cultural "impoverishment" relative to their aboriginal state. Their own culture was changing, but they had not yet been exposed directly to the alternatives that the Spanish, French, and English were to provide after 1673. Thus the drastic changes that took place during the period 1540–1673 in the interior placed the natives in a position that enabled them more easily to accept elements of European culture reaching them after 1673, when acculturation truly began.

7

The Aftermath: Toward the

Formation of the Creek Confederacy

In 1894, J. N. B. Hewitt stated, "No league or confederation of peoples was perhaps ever formed without a sufficient motive in the nature of outside pressure." The Creek Confederacy was formed out of the tribal remnants of once powerful chiefdoms—which had already disintegrated under indirect European influence (primarily disease)—in response to new outside pressures of the seventeenth century. An attempt will be made to demonstrate that the confederacy was formed in response to armed incursions of northern native groups and pressure from European slave traders in the middle to late seventeenth century.

John R. Swanton suggested that the Creek Confederacy was in existence at the time of de Soto (1922:257). Unfortunately, Swanton never really understood the political reality of the sixteenth-century Southeast. What he mistook for the Creek Confederacy was in actuality one or more complex chiefdoms (i.e., those with several tiers of a multitown hierarchy). Similarly, David Corkran (1967) discusses the "Upper" and "Lower" Creeks in the sixteenth century, terms which the Indians would not use till well over a century later. Vernon J. Knight correctly points out that the term "Creek" was not in general use even in 1700 (Knight and Adams 1981:48). Swanton did report that William Bartram recorded a traditional belief that the Creek Confederacy had originated at the old town of Ocmulgee in central Georgia (1928:262). Finally, Verner Crane believed that the Yamassee War and the subsequent migration of Indians away from the South Carolina border "promoted a further amalgamation of tribes, Muskhogean and non-Muskhogean, into that remarkable league, the

Creek Confederation" (1981:254). I will attempt to demonstrate an earlier formation of the Creek Confederacy as well as an archaeological correlate of the confederation process.

In *Europe and the People without History,* Eric Wolf points out that there were broad connections across large segments of the world. Europeans had economic ties with China, and there were broad, long-range connections operating in the New World. From this viewpoint, it is no longer appropriate to look at the Southeast as an isolated area in the seventeenth century. To understand the formation of the Creek Confederacy, it is necessary to look at the interior Southeast as a part of a larger, highly dynamic system. Paraphrasing Hewitt, then, the Creek Confederacy was formed as a response to external pressures. To understand its formation, it is necessary to set the stage.

First let us consider the European presence in the New World from the middle to the late seventeenth century. In the Southeast, the Spaniards occupied St. Augustine and a chain of missions up the Georgia coast and across northern Florida. In 1686, Marcos Delgado was sent into the interior to look for LaSalle, and in 1689 the Spaniards constructed Fort Apalachicola on the Chattahoochee River just south of the fall line in present Russell County, Alabama (DeJarnette 1975:200–203).

The English had settled farther north, founding Jamestown in 1607. It quickly became important in the Indian trade, and the Virginia traders Needham and Arthur reached the Tennessee Valley by 1673 (Williams 1928). With the founding of Charles Towne in 1670, English-Indian trade intensified and slave trading rapidly became important (Wright 1981). The founding of Charles Town would have a serious impact on southeastern Indians (Crane 1981).

Farther north, the English founded the Plymouth colony in 1620 and took over New York from the Dutch in 1664, ending over fifty years of Dutch influence, which had begun in 1609 with the voyage of Henry Hudson.

French history in the New World was somewhat different. After failing to establish colonies in South Carolina and Florida in the sixteenth century, French interest centered on the St. Lawrence River area and spread throughout the Great Lakes region during the seventeenth century. By 1673, Marquette and Joliet were descending the Mississippi, and later LaSalle continued their explorations, discovering the mouth of the river and even attempting to colonize the coast of Texas. Arkansas Post and Illinois settlements were established in the 1680s (Sauer 1980).

By the 1680s, the Indians of the interior eastern woodlands were thus surrounded by the ever-tightening noose of the European presence. The differing colonial interests of these European groups exerted severe pressure on native American groups.

As discussed in chapters 4 and 5, the Indians of the interior Southeast had declined in number and their political organization had disintegrated from highly organized, complex chiefdoms to smaller units. Population movements resulted from the natives' desire to flee diseased areas and from shifts in the balance of power among aboriginal groups. But some of the major changes were yet to come. Remembering that the overall picture of colonial North America is important in understanding the dynamics of the study area, we must first turn to the Indians of the Northeast.

To oversimplify a complex situation, the seventeenth-century Northeast can be viewed as a struggle between France's Indian allies and those of the Dutch (or the English after 1664). The major antagonists were the French-supported Huron of Ontario and the Dutch-supported Five Nations Iroquois (Seneca, Onondaga, Oneida, Cayuga, and Mohawk) of New York. These were large confederacies of tribal groups, probably banded together because of the political necessity of dealing with Europeans. To the south lay the powerful Susquehannocks in Pennsylvania, supplied by the Dutch in New York, the Swedes, and the English in Chesapeake Bay.

The Iroquois wars are perhaps best viewed as basically a European fight (fought through Indian allies) over valuable furs (Trigger 1978: 352–54). Trade in furs had been going on along the coast of the northeast in the early sixteenth century, and by 1535 Jacques Cartier had sailed up the St. Lawrence River well into interior Canada. Explorations by Champlain and Henry Hudson in 1609 created intense competition. Champlain aided Indian allies against the Iroquois (Mohawk) in 1609 and 1610 and in 1615 helped the Huron on a raid against one of the central tribes of the Iroquois confederacy (Trigger 1978:348–49). From that point on, the struggle intensified. The Dutch, a more industrial group than the French (Wolf 1982:115–20), were better able to supply their Indian allies with firearms, and by around 1640 the Seneca, farthest west of the Five Nations, had acquired guns (Wray 1973:9). Soon after, the Iroquois began to overrun their neighbors. The details of the Iroquois wars are not important here (see Hunt 1940; Trigger 1978) but the results are. In 1638 the Wenro were forced to move, and in 1649–50 the Petun were dispersed. There followed the destruction of the Neutral in 1652, the

Erie in 1654–56, and the Susquehannocks in 1675 (actually brought about by an attack from Europeans from Maryland and Virginia [Trigger 1978:356]).

What is important to this study are the population movements caused by the Iroquois wars. Several groups moved south: some of the Neutral moved into the Ohio River Valley (Trigger 1978:355); the Erie, in a number of steps, eventually ended up in Georgia; many Susquehannocks settled in Maryland. One group of Susquehannocks, however, moved all the way to Ocaneechi Island in the Roanoke River near the Virginia–North Carolina border (Jennings 1978:366).

The travels of the Erie have been much debated. Originally, they were located along the southeastern shore of Lake Erie in the present states of New York and Pennsylvania (White 1978:412–13). Following their dispersion by the Iroquois in 1654–56 (the exact date is not known due to a lapse in the Jesuit relations), the location of the Erie is unknown. A group of some six hundred surrendered to the Iroquois near Virginia, according to the Jesuit narratives, and Marian White notes that "Virginia" of the time meant to the French "an uncharted region down the Ohio across the mountains and below Pennsylvania" (1978:416).

Others believe that the Erie (or part of the tribe) moved farther south, where they show up as the Richahecrians, a strange Indian group who appeared briefly to menace western Virginia in 1656 (Hoffman 1964; Hunter 1978:588; Wright 1981:6, 87). This identification, based on the coincidence of the date and the closeness of the name Rickahecrian as recorded by the English to the Erie name Riqueronnons or Riquehronnons recorded by the French, seems reasonable, especially when combined with the information from the Jesuit Relations that the Erie moved south. But this was only a temporary stop.

Both Crane (1981:6) and Mason (1963) identify the Westo, who settled on the Georgia side of the Savannah River near present Augusta, as the Rickohockans of Virginia fame (there are several variations in spelling) and consequently as the Erie. They first appeared in the Deep South as "Chichimecas," who attacked Guale in 1661 from the north (Crane 1981:5), and were mentioned as the Westo as early as 1670 (Swanton 1922:66) in the Carolina colony records. Crane believed that the Westo had been armed with firearms while in Virginia (1981:12), but it is likely that they had obtained firearms while they were still in the Northeast; their defeat by the Iroquois was blamed on the fact that they ran out of ammunition (White 1978:412). Whatever their source of firearms, they terrorized the local southeastern Indians, who would not have firearms for several more years.

Part of Crane's identification of the Westo as a northern group rests on the description of their settlement by Henry Woodward in 1674 as a palisaded village of long bark houses. This community plan is not native to the Southeast and definitely suggests a northern origin for the Westo, although it does not necessarily demonstrate that they were the Erie.

From this contact in 1674 until 1680, the Westo were strongly allied with South Carolina, which provided guns and ammunition to raid Spanish Indians, and by 1680 raids were being made into Guale under English incitement (Crane 1981:17). Eventually relations between South Carolina and the Westo deteriorated, leading to the Westo war, and by 1683 they were defeated and scattered, a remnant group finally settling as a town in the Lower Creek country (Crane 1981:20).

Because the Westo operated on the western fringe of the new Carolina colony, they are documented. Probably numerous other groups in the interior were equally disruptive. Without a direct European presence, such activity is unrecorded, but there is additional evidence for such movements, both historical and archaeological.

After the French descended the Mississippi River in 1682, the Spaniards began to worry about the invasion of their territory in the Southeast. In 1686, Marcos Delgado was sent into the interior to meet this perceived French threat (Boyd 1937). He went no further than the area of the junction of the Coosa and Tallapoosa rivers, where he stayed with various native groups, and left a remarkable record of the aboriginal settlement dynamics of the area.

Delgado reports that five groups of northern Indians had recently settled in that area, fleeing from the English and Chichimecas from the north (Boyd 1937:21, 26). It should be noted that "Chichimeca" is a term used to designate wild, warlike tribes in general, being used (actually originating) in northern Mexico as well as the Southeast. That is, Delgado's Chichimecas were not necessarily the same group of that name that was terrorizing the Guale area at about the same time; that is, they may or may not have been the Westo. What is important is that they came from the north. Their possession of firearms, attributable to their association with the English, gave them the power to force the movement of unarmed refugee groups to the south.

In addition to the "Chichimecas," Delgado mentions another nation called Chalaque, which was responsible for forcing population movements south. Boyd (1937:32) equates them with the Cherokee, but it should be noted that the word "Chalaque" is probably a corruption of the Muskhogean word "čilo·kkita," which means "people of a different language" (Hudson et al. 1984), therefore not necessarily the Cherokee. On the other hand, archaeological evidence from the Tellico Reservoir shows a sudden influx of Period D European artifacts at sites such as Citico and Toqua. This influx probably marks the entrance into the Little Tennessee River Valley of the Overhill Cherokee. There is little doubt that the Overhill were latecomers to the valley, because the names recorded by the chroniclers of the de Soto and Pardo expeditions in this area are all Muskhogean (Hudson et al. 1985; Charles Hudson, personal communication).

Delgado mentions two other northern groups by name: the Quasate (whom Boyd equates with the Koasati) and the Tubani of the Quasate Nation. He also mentions the Pagna, the Qulasa of the province of Pagna, and the Aymamu, who were said to have fled the Chata (whom Boyd equates with the Choctaw), suggesting a western origin (Boyd 1937:26). If these three groups are part of the five groups that Delgado had mentioned, it is clear that English influence had reached the "Chata." Since the Choctaw were never influenced heavily by the English, it is unlikely that the "chata" of Delgado were the later Choctaw. Nonetheless, the Aymamu can be identified with the Alabamu of the de Soto period and late eighteenth century, as Boyd notes, and these people were definitely located to the northwest of the Coosa-Tallapoosa junction area. Delgado's report also makes it clear that the English had been in the province of Apalachicola and that the people of the Coosa-Tallapoosa area were at war with the Mobile Indians farther down the Alabama River.

It is important to see the overall pattern indicated by these two isolated cases, documented by chance. First, many northern groups, usually armed with firearms obtained from the French, Dutch, and English, were moving toward the south. Historical evidence that Huron, Susquehannock, and Erie all moved south has been mentioned, and these armed groups probably then caused displacements of unarmed groups farther south, causing a chain of serial movements southward. Thus, Delgado recorded refugees from the north in the area of the junction of the Coosa and Tallapoosa rivers, and the Westo were attacking the Guale in the 1680s. It is these refugee groups who were moving during the last third of the seventeenth century, the remnants of once powerful chiefdoms, that eventually became what was known as the Creek Confederacy during the eighteenth century. The outside pressures responsible for the formation of the Creek Confederacy can be summed up as firearms and the slave trade.

Firearms were the main catalyst in the process which, for our purposes, culminated in the formation of the Creek Confederacy. Matchlocks were brought into eastern North America from Florida to Canada with the earliest explorers in the sixteenth century. However, it was not until about 1625, with the perfection of the flintlock, that guns became everyday tools in the New World and goods for the Indian trade (Hamilton 1980:9). The Indians always wanted firearms, and they were obtaining guns in Virginia by 1623 (Wright 1981:69, 303), through either trade or warfare; they were said to be as skilled in the use of firearms as the English colonists were. However, the real center of the gun trade was the northern fur-producing areas of New York and Ontario. Here the Dutch, English, Swedes, and French all competed for valuable furs. While trade in firearms was frequently against the law, some enterprising trader was always willing to sell guns to the Indians. The Dutch provided an abundance of firearms to their Iroquois allies. Even the westernmost group of the Five Nations Iroquois, the Seneca, were heavily armed by the 1640s (Wray 1973), and they were able to destroy virtually all of their neighbors by 1675, causing population displacements.

The firearm situation in the South was different. There was no competition between European nations for valuable furs during the sixteenth and seventeenth centuries. Spain was not a heavily industrialized nation (Wolf 1982), and the Spaniards simply made it their policy not to trade guns to the Indians (Smith 1956:106). Indians in the Deep South were therefore unarmed and at the mercy of armed Indian groups from the North. Once population movements were set into motion by the Iroquois wars and more and more groups were armed by Virginia traders and, after 1670, Carolina traders, the shock wave of increased warfare moved across the South.

This was a new kind of warfare, based on access to goods desired by European traders: deerskins and slaves in the Southeast. During the late seventeenth century, slaves were probably the more important commodity. The English wanted Indian slaves to be transshipped to Caribbean islands for plantation labor (Wright 1981). By arming Indian groups on their western frontiers, Virginia and Carolina traders could be assured of a steady supply of slaves.

The desire to capture slaves and the military advantage conferred by firearms thus combined to terrorize the Indians of the study area by the last third of the seventeenth century. This pressure caused vast

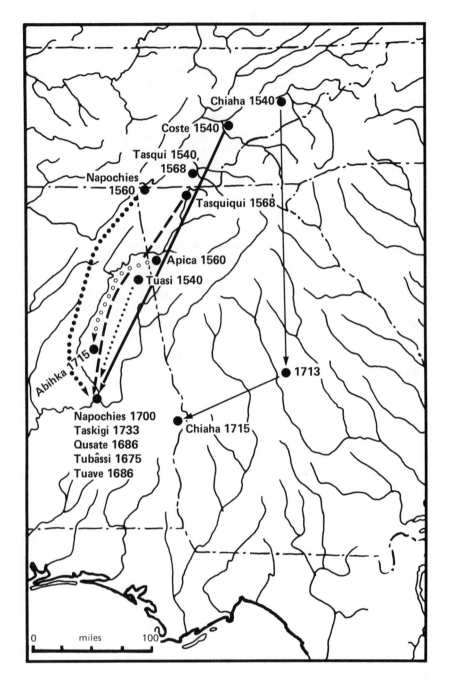

Figure 7.1. Seventeenth-century population movements.

population movements and forced the birth of the Creek Confederacy, a political expedient of unarmed refugee groups banding together for survival. While population movements during the early historic period have been demonstrated, they were usually of relatively short distance, probably to escape diseased areas. Population movements in the late seventeenth century, however, were long-range movements either to escape armed groups (the earliest major movements, such as those noted by Delgado) or to move closer to English traders to obtain firearms (such as the movement of several towns from the Chatta-hoochee to the Ocmulgee in the 1680s [Swanton 1946:143]).

Figure 7.1 illustrates some of these long-distance movements. Migration routes that seem secure are shown as solid lines, while dashed lines link documented locations of different time periods when the route of migration is uncertain. The movement of Coosa down the Coosa drainage is fairly secure (fig. 4.2), but the movement of Chiaha and Coste is not as well understood (fig. 7.1). We know their locations in the sixteenth century and at the beginning of the eighteenth century, but intermediate steps are not clear. These two groups might have moved in the late seventeenth century in rather large leaps to flee armed groups coming from the north and east. Such a move is verified in the Delgado document for Koasati (i.e., Qusate or Coste). Chiaha is known to have been on the Ocmulgee in 1713 and soon thereafter moved to the Chattahoochee (Swanton 1946:115–16). The leap from northern Tennessee to the Ocmulgee is not known. It is even possible that they had first settled on the Chattahoochee and later moved east with the Coweta and Kasihta.

The movement of the Apica (i.e., Abihka of the eighteenth century) probably paralleled that of the Coosa. Apica was part of that chiefdom and in the eighteenth century was closely related to Coosa, surpassing it in importance by the end of the century. The Apica were still located near Rome, Georgia (probably the Johnstone Farm site), in the 1560s when Luna's men visited them, but archaeological evidence suggests that they moved south soon thereafter.

Other movements away from the de Soto–Luna–Pardo period locations had taken place by 1700. The Tuasi village of the de Soto period was probably located at the junction of Nances Creek and Terrapin Creek in Cherokee County, Alabama (DePratter et al. 1985) at site 1Ce308 (Little and Curren 1981). In 1675, Bishop Calderon listed a group, the Tubâssi, with the Coosa-Tallapoosa towns (Wenhold 1936:10). In 1686, Marcos Delgado reported the town of Tuave near the junction of the Coosa and Tallapoosa rivers.

The Tasqui mentioned by Ranjel in 1540 and Bandera in 1568 were located in present eastern Tennessee, probably near the present town of Conasauga (DePratter et al. 1985). They were not mentioned again until they appear on Levasseur's town list of 1700 as the Tascqui, a group on the Coosa or Tallapoosa River in Alabama (Knight and Adams 1981). Since they did not appear on Calderon's 1675 list or in the Delgado accounts of 1686, they likely were recent arrivals in Alabama.

A related group, the Tasquiqui, were said by Bandera in 1568 to be located a short distance beyond Tasqui on the trail to Coosa (DePratter et al. 1983:149). That is, Tasquiqui was probably located in extreme northern Georgia on the upper Conasauga River. It may have been the small village mentioned in the de Soto narratives the day after Tasqui. John Swanton (1922:209) notes that the early eighteenth-century maps by Homann and Seale place "Tuskegee" near the headwaters of the Coosa, or precisely where it was in the sixteenth century, and he interprets this placement as evidence to suggest that "the migration of the Alabama Tuskegee southward was a comparatively late movement, something which took place late in the seventeenth century or early in the eighteenth."

On the Couvens and Mortier map of the early eighteenth century, the Tuskegee were located north of the Abihka on the Coosa River (Swanton 1922:209), and DeCrenay located them on his 1733 map at the junction of the Coosa and Tallapoosa. Swanton also notes that branches of the Tuskegee were located at various times in Tennessee, on the Chattahoochee, and perhaps even on the Ocmulgee River (1922:208–11). Considering that maps frequently incorporate out-of-date information, it is suggested that beginning in the seventeenth century the main group of Tasquiqui moved south along the Coosa drainage to end up at the junction of the Coosa and Tallapoosa rivers prior to 1733.

The Napochies also ended up near the junction of the Coosa and Tallapoosa. As discussed, they can be located near present Chattanooga, Tennessee, in 1560. Although the archaeological evidence is weak, I have suggested that they moved farther down the Tennessee River into Alabama to the Pine Island area around 1630. They reappeared in 1700 on Levasseur's town list of Alabama-Coosa-Tallapoosa river groups as the Napachés (Knight and Adams 1981:51). Vernon J. Knight (personal communication) states, "The Barnwell MS map of ca. 1722 has a town, opposite Ft. Toulouse, which seems to be 'Nabootche.'. . . It is next to Pakana, an Alibamu town, and it disappears on such derivative maps as Popple's of 1733. It is not on French maps of the 1730s either, so if the identification is right, they seem to be finally extinct or absorbed by that time." The hypothesized collapse of the chiefdom of Ocute into the eighteenth-century Oconee Old Town has been discussed (fig. 4.2).

These movements demonstrate the disruption brought about by the collapse of high-level political integration, population decline, and outside pressure. Historical evidence suggests that political reorganization was well under way by 1686. The formation of the Creek Confederacy probably took place over time, beginning as a series of small alliances. One example will suffice. If the Tuave mentioned by Delgado in 1686 were the descendants of de Soto's Tuasi, they had been located in the sixteenth century on Terrapin Creek in northeastern Alabama and were part of the province of Coosa (DePratter et al. 1985). Delgado says that the Tuave were a village of the Cosate, whom we can equate with Coste of the de Soto narratives. During the sixteenth century, the Coste were located far to the north on Bussell Island in the Tennessee River of Eastern Tennessee (DePratter et al. 1985) and were affiliated with Coosa. Thus in the sixteenth century these two groups were located some 160 miles apart, but by the late seventeenth century they were closely affiliated and had relocated hundreds of miles to the south.

Three of the four tribes of importance in the Creek Confederacy in the eighteenth century (Coweta, Kasihta, Tuckabatchee, and Coosa, according to Corkran 1967:4) avoided direct European contact until the late seventeenth century. The exception, Coosa, had been a powerful complex chiefdom during the sixteenth century and was no doubt still an important group because of its former glory. Tuckabatchee was located near the fall line on the Tallapoosa River in the eighteenth century and probably had been in that general location since the fifteenth century (Vernon Knight, personal communication). Early European exploration bypassed the Tallapoosa drainage, concentrating instead on the Coosa (DePratter et al. 1985). Thus, perhaps Tuckabatchee was spared some of the disease and starvation that ravaged areas that faced direct European contact by de Soto and Luna. (De Soto in particular was very hard on the native population—stealing stored food, taking carriers and women, and even murdering Indians from time to time.) Likewise the Kasihta and Coweta, probably located along the Chattahoochee River in prehistory (Vernon Knight, personal communication), were able to maintain their precontact vigor until a later period and were spared the horrors of European contact until the coming of English traders from Charles Towne. After 1680 both towns (formerly simple chiefdoms?) moved to the Ocmulgee River to be nearer to English traders who supplied them with guns, but following the Yamassee War in 1715 they returned to the Chattahoochee (Swanton 1946).

What does the archaeological record tell us about these hypothesized events? Is there any archaeological evidence for increased north-south interaction, and are there archaeological correlates for the Creek Confederacy?

There is some archaeological evidence for late seventeenth-century interaction with more northerly groups. It is in the form of glass bead types identical or similar to types known to have been manufactured in Holland (Karklins 1974, 1984) and commonly traded in the Northeast. These types (IVb33 and IVnn4; Kidd and Kidd 1970) are quite common in seventeenth-century sites in New York (Pratt 1961; Bradley 1979) and Maryland (Ferguson 1940) and even as far south as northern North Carolina (Wilson 1980), but they are virtually unknown from areas of Spanish influence. Two late seventeenth-century sites in Alabama, however, have produced these beads in limited quantities. Site 1Ms32 in the Guntersville Reservoir has produced a blue and white striped bead of Kidd type IVb33 (fig. 7.2) (Moundville collections). This site has been assigned to Period D, 1630–70 (chapter 3). From the second site, near the Cooper Farm site near Gadsden, Alabama, a large copper or brass axe effigy has been reported with a burial (Greer 1966) as well as a large red, white, and blue striped chevron bead of Kidd type IVnn4 (fig. 7.2) (E. S. Greer, personal communication). This poorly known site is placed in the late seventeenth century, but it may date to Period D. Bead type IVnn4 has been found in glass factory refuse in Amsterdam (Karklins 1984), and type IVb33 is virtually identical to type IVb34, which is also found in Amsterdam. Only the spacing of the stripes varies: IVb33 has paired stripes, IVb34 has evenly spaced stripes. Both IVb33 and IVb34 are common on Iroquois sites in the Northeast; the absence of IVb33 in the Dutch factory collections is probably due to sampling error.

The fact that only one or two of these beads has been found on a limited number of sites in the Southeast does not suggest that there was a change in source of supply to the European traders. Rather, it suggests that there was increased interaction (raiding?) between Indians of the Northeast and the Southeast. The Great Indian Warpath down the Tennessee Valley documented by Myer (1928) was no doubt an old "interaction" route. Clearly, the two sites in Alabama were not

0 _____ 1
      cm

Figure 7.2. Dutch glass beads: *left*, IVnn4; *right*, IVb33.

sites of northern Indians who moved south but of indigenous groups who had infrequent access to Dutch trade goods. Only a glance at the aboriginal material from those sites is necessary to confirm their identity.

What about archaeological correlates of the Creek Confederacy? It is argued that the sudden appearance of a ceramic horizon style, dominated by the type Chattahoochee Brushed or its shell-tempered equivalent Walnut Roughened marks the formation of the Creek Confederacy.

The origins of brushed pottery has been debated for years. Charles Fairbanks originally believed that the type was derived from the Lamar stamping tradition of central Georgia, a sort of degenerate complicated stamped type (Fairbanks 1952:298; 1958). Later Roy S. Dickens (1979), working at the Horseshoe Bend site in Alabama, suggested that it was derived from an earlier Dadeville series in Alabama. More recently, Vernon J. Knight has suggested the presence of a sixteenth- and seventeenth-century brushed ware in the Tallapoosa drainage, part of his Atasi Complex (Knight and Smith 1980). The present consensus seems to favor an origin in eastern Alabama.

Whatever its origin, the type quickly spread across the southeastern piedmont along the fall line. In addition to sites mentioned on the Tallapoosa drainage, Chattahoochee Brushed pottery is common on the Chattahoochee (DeJarnette 1975), the Ocmulgee (Fairbanks 1952; Smith 1973), and the Oconee at the Oconee Old Town site (Williams 1983). It is my thesis here that the sudden spread of this style can be traced back to population movements triggered by the late seventeenth-century warfare and slave raiding by armed groups to the north. As refugee groups banded together for protection, group intermarriage occurred. Increasing population movements, such as the documented movement of Kasihta and Coweta to the Ocmulgee River in the 1680s, helped to spread the style to the east. All these movements and accompanying intermarriages lead to a homogenization of ceramic styles, and the result was the brushed horizon style. This style is the hallmark of the increased interaction that was the result of the formation of the Creek Confederacy. The fact that many of the sites that share this horizon style were located along the main English trading path (Goff 1953) is also significant. James Deetz (1965:99) has demonstrated a trend in Arikara ceramics toward standardization over time as the Arikara underwent depopulation and subsequent village consolidation.

In conclusion, it is proposed that the depopulation and decentralization of sixteenth-century chiefdoms in the study area led to increasing recombinations of refugee groups. This process was accelerated during the second half of the seventeenth century by external pressures from displaced northeastern aboriginal groups who had firearms and from slave hunters, both Europeans and their Indian allies. These pressures were one of the major factors leading to the formation of that well-known eighteenth-century entity, the Creek Confederacy. An early stage of the confederacy was evident in the lower Coosa–Tallapoosa River area by the last quarter of the seventeenth century. Marcos Delgado reported settlement of refugee groups near the headwaters of the Alabama River in 1686, and William Bartram recorded a Creek legend that the confederacy was formed at Ocmulgee town in central Georgia while the Kasihta and Coweta were in the area (around 1689–1715). Milfort (1972:114–15) records a tradition of the Creek that "an Indian tribe, which had just been almost destroyed by the Iroquois and the Hurons, came to request the protection of the Moskoquis, which I shall now call Creeks. The latter received them among themselves and assigned them a piece of land in the center of their nation. They built a town which is rather large, which is called Tuket-Batchet." These documented events were separate manifestations of the same process. The refugees of the earlier chiefdoms found it necessary to form a political alliance so that they could deal with outside pressures brought about by the fur trade wars in the North and the slave trade in the South.

8

Final Considerations and Future Research

USING archaeological and historical data from a portion of the interior Southeast, I have attempted to elucidate the process of the disintegration of chiefdoms following contact with Europeans in the sixteenth century. A model of disintegration suggested by several students of the New World was developed and tested with data from the study area.

A chronology based on European trade goods was developed in order to measure the rate of change from chiefdom to nonchiefdom. It was needed to provide the tight chronological control necessary to determine the timing of the changes during the early historic period. Several different archaeological measures were used to document the demographic collapse that took place during this period. Using multiple burials as an indicator of European disease epidemics, it was possible to show that disease was an important factor during Periods A (1540–65), and C (1600–1630). Period A covers the direct European contact of the de Soto and Luna expeditions as well as the time in which the possible effects of earlier pandemics from coastal contacts would begin to appear in the archaeological record. Data from Period B (1565–1600) were not sufficient for conclusions to be made. Contact with the Pardo expeditions of 1566–68 probably spread more disease into the interior, and pandemics may have spread inland from St. Augustine, Santa Elena, and the coastal Guale missions. There are some archaeological data to show that during Period C (1600–1630) the practice of multiple burial was again important, suggesting the presence of disease epidemics. It is precisely the period when a sudden influx of European goods appears in the study area.

Evidence for decreases in site size was also sought as an indicator

143

of depopulation. While difficult to obtain, data from the Coosa, Tennessee, and Oconee River drainages showed a clear trend toward such decreases. They began during Period A, suggesting the early impact of disease epidemics. Mean site size in the Wallace Reservoir decreased from the sixteenth to the seventeenth century.

Settlement counts, also used as an indicator of depopulation, showed a decrease from Period A to B, a stabilization or increase from Period B to C, and a decrease to Period D. The apparent stabilization or increase from Period B to C is probably an artifact of the lack of data for Period B. Wallace Reservoir data also showed a substantial decline in the number of components from the sixteenth to the seventeenth century.

It was hypothesized that under the stress of depopulation, sites would be abandoned and new sites established. Clear movements of population down the Coosa River were demonstrated, and although precise movements cannot be as easily determined from the Tennessee or Oconee River areas, site abandonment and the founding of new sites in these areas show that the same type of movement was occurring. Such movements began during the sixteenth century, again suggesting devastating effects of early epidemics.

Several indicators of the decline of chiefly organization were also developed and tested with data from the study area. The end of mound construction was believed to be a possible signal of the end of chiefly authority. The data suggest that no mounds were begun after 1600, that perhaps mound construction had ceased as early as the end of Period A (1565), and that no mounds were added to after 1630 in the study area. By Period D (1630–70), no mound centers were even occupied by groups that could be demonstrated to have built them. Available data thus suggest that chiefly power was severely eroded by the late sixteenth century.

The construction of palisades, another type of public work, was also considered a correlate of chiefly power. A length-to-width ratio of site dimensions was developed to indicate the presence of palisades where direct evidence was lacking. It showed that palisades were not constructed in the study area after Period C (1630).

The elaborate hierarchy of sites mentioned in the de Soto documents and demonstrated archaeologically also disintegrated rapidly. In the Oconee River drainage, the elaborate prehistoric site hierarchy was gone by 1600.

Studies of burial practices, especially the inclusion of types of sociotechnic markers commonly in use during the prehistoric period, showed that chiefly organization eroded quickly. Stone spatulate axes and native copper artifacts were often both absent by around 1610. Other possible indicators of the loss of chiefly organization were mentioned, but the archaeological data are not available to test them.

Craft specialization was also viewed as an indicator of a chiefdom level of organization. Native copper and spatulate axes disappeared by the early seventeenth century, but Citico-style rattlesnake gorgets may have persisted in use for another twenty years. Thus, most traits that were suggested to correspond to a chiefdom type of organization can be shown to have disappeared by about the beginning of the seventeenth century—certainly no later than the first third of the century.

The fact that the demise of chiefly organization corresponds almost exactly with the evidence for depopulation is no accident. It has been demonstrated that acculturation was not a factor in culture change during the early historic period but that, nonetheless, a great deal of change had taken place. It was a process of "deculturation," or loss of cultural elements, as discussed by Steward and Faron (1959:176). There can be no doubt that the primary cause of culture change during this period was depopulation brought about by European disease epidemics. So few people were left that chiefly organization could not be maintained: there were not enough workers in the labor force to provide a food surplus to support it, and there were not enough warriors to conduct the warfare that had characterized chiefdoms (DePratter 1983). Public works were no longer constructed, craft specialists were no longer supported, and quite possibly ritual specialists died off faster than they could transmit their esoteric knowledge (Hudson 1980). The early historic period was a time of collapse; that collapse appeared by the beginning of the seventeenth century, leaving the southeastern Indians in a state of "cultural impoverishment" and leading to the rapid acculturation that took place during the eighteenth century.

Remnants of the once-powerful chiefdoms, now reduced to little more than small towns, banded together for mutual defense from incursions of armed Indians from the north and slave traders from the east. Thus the Creek Confederacy was formed as a response to outside pressures that could no longer be withstood. Similar groupings were taking place in chiefdoms all over the Western hemisphere.

Much work remains to be done. Period B (1565–1600) is the least understood period in the sequence, yet it appears to be the time of greatest change. New sites were being settled and old sites abandoned;

mound building ceased, and site-specific settlement patterns were changing from compact, palisaded towns to more dispersed, linear villages. The contrast between sites of Period A and of Period C is clear, but sites of Period B must be excavated to understand this shift. We need particularly to have burial data to confirm or deny the presence of disease epidemics and to demonstrate the shift from ascribed to achieved status. If such a shift did indeed take place at that time, there should be a random pattern in the distribution of grave goods instead of the clustering that would be expected with an ascribed system of ranked clans. More town plans must be examined to understand the shift in settlement patterns.

Shifts in subsistence during the early historic period are also poorly understood. Faunal analysts are thus far silent on the impact of the swine distributed by de Soto. Evidence has been presented that peaches were being grown in the interior by 1630, and it is suspected that this date will eventually be pushed back into the sixteenth century as more data are analyzed. It may be possible to detect a shift toward a fur- or leather-hunting economy by the end of the early historic period. While many of the European artifacts found on sites of the period may have been gifts to cement political alliances, trading was probably becoming more and more important. Again, this change should be detectable archaeologically, perhaps by seeing an increase in the remains of economically important fauna, such as deer or fur-bearing animals.

While several possible population movements during the early historic period have been suggested here, these movements should be taken as hypotheses and further tested. We need to look for specific, traceable aboriginal traits to show group continuity from one site to another. This will be difficult to demonstrate, especially because families (and thus craftspersons) were dying at an alarming rate. Resettlement of survivors and amalgamation of refugees will make particular towns difficult to trace, but it should be possible to do so through diligent study of aboriginal traits.

The early historic period was a time of great change throughout the New World. It has been made clear here that the direct historic approach—working from well-described eighteenth-century groups back to the time of contact—is bound to fail to describe what was happening in the interior of the Southeast. Far too much disruption had been brought about by catastrophic depopulation during the historic period. Groups moved, refugees regrouped, and cultures were severely altered, making the Southeast of the eighteenth century a very different place than its prehistoric forerunner. The prehistoric Southeast was a complicated area of highly developed chiefdoms. Unfortunately, after the disruptions of the early historic period, we are left with only the meager descriptions of the sixteenth-century explorers and archaeological data to try to unravel these complexities. Sadly, this is also the case for much of the New World.

It is intended that this study stimulate more research into the processes of the decline of the New World chiefdoms brought about by the European conquest. Better archaeological data must be collected to refine the model presented here. A regional approach should be utilized for intensive study of particular chiefdoms. Basic data such as site size must be collected for more locales. Extensive excavation of particular sites should be made and the frequency of mass and multiple burials examined. Physical anthropologists should study large skeletal series to look for population curves suggestive of disease epidemics and for the presence of people of mixed European-African-Indian ancestry. Indeed, it should eventually be possible to find the burials of European explorers. The early historic period was a time of great change; understanding the processes of this change is a challenge for historians, ethnohistorians, and archaeologists. We are only beginning to understand the dramatic collapse that took place.

Appendix 1

Additional Site Data

Bob Johnstone Farm (9Fl49)

The Johnstone Farm Site, believed to be the sixteenth-century Apica town site, has never been investigated by archaeologists. All data on this important site were derived from an avid collector, Steve Hunter, the landowner, and from a short reconnaissance of the site by David Hally and me in August 1984. Steve Hunter claims to have excavated approximately seventy-six burials from the site during the early 1970s, but he kept no notes and did not catalog his collection. At least three burials recovered by Hunter contained European artifacts. The burial of a young child contained a necklace of shell beads with two rolled sheet copper or brass beads of apparent European metal. In the same "burial plot," perhaps a house area, Hunter recovered a "male" burial with three pieces of iron: a large chisel-ended rod, 230 mm long by 28 mm diameter; a rectangular iron celt 135 mm long, 33 mm wide, and 22 mm thick (before cleaning); and a small iron pin 119 mm long, 12 mm wide, and 5 mm thick. A third burial, apparently from another area, yielded an iron knob, probably the hilt of a sword similar to that on the sword from the King site. Additional grave goods recovered by Hunter from other burials include Citico-style rattlesnake gorgets, a mask gorget, pottery vessels including Lamar Coarse Plain strap-handled Mississippian jars, projectile point caches, and a small, leaf-shaped knife.

A reconnaissance trip to the site in 1984 showed evidence of active vandalism. Although crops were in the fields, precluding surface collecting, vandalism in the wooded strip adjacent to the river extended approximately 400 feet (estimated from 135 paces), and vandalism on the adjacent wooded property indicated a minimum site width of approximately 120 feet perpendicular to the river. A collection of ceramics from vandalized areas, is now curated at the University of Georgia. It includes Lamar Incised, Lamar Stamped, and shell-tempered Dallas types, indicating a Barnett phase occupation. The presence of large quantities of daub and burned posts in the spoil dirt indicates that many houses burned. Human remains adjacent to many potholes indicate that numerous burials had been disturbed.

The available data suggest that the Johnstone Farm was much like the King site in terms of ceramics, grave goods, and burned houses. It covers an area minimally 400 by 120 feet and was probably much larger. Clearly it was a village-sized community, not a hamlet. This important site should be investigated by professional archaeologists to determine its exact size and the presence of fortifications and to obtain a larger ceramic sample.

Brown Farm (9Go67)

The Brown Farm village site is located on property of the Moss Land Company in the final bend of the Coosawattee River before its confluence with the Conasauga River. It is known primarily through the efforts of collector Steve Hunter, who reports excavating approximately seventy burials, two of which contained European artifacts. One burial contained a shell masklike gorget, 200–300 small shell beads around the neck and down the arm, two well-made, long projectile points, a poorly preserved possible antler flaker, a small flaring-rim jar about 4 inches in diameter, and two pieces of iron. One piece of iron was a long rod measuring 144 mm long by 9 mm in diameter, with chisel-like end; the other was a small celt (?) 68 mm long, 36 mm wide, and 8 mm thick. A second burial contained a mass of fish teeth (species: drum) and a clay bead (the remains of a rattle?) on the right arm and an oval piece of iron 87 mm long, 38 mm wide, and 1–2 mm thick, located under the chin. This unidentified iron object, perhaps a knife blade, may have served as a gorget.

This site was also visited by David Hally and me in August 1984 and again by me in December 1984. Site size was estimated (by pacing) as 650 by 600 feet. A small surface collection of Barnett phase pottery was made and is currently curated at the University of Georgia. Discussions with the tenant disclosed that digging proceeds during the portions of the year when the field is not in crops. According to Steve Hunter, a spatulate axe was recovered recently from this site by another collector.

Terrapin Creek

The Terrapin Creek site is a large village located at the confluence of Terrapin Creek and the Coosa River in Cherokee County, Alabama. It has not been investigated by professional archaeologists but has received considerable attention from collectors. An undetermined number of burials have been excavated from this large village site, at least sixteen of which contained European artifacts typical of the turn of the sixteenth century. Interviews with collectors and firsthand study of their collections yielded some information, and an inventory of the glass beads recovered is presented in table A.1.

Burial 1 was a "tiny baby" located about 30 inches beneath the surface. Some 85 glass beads were sprinkled over the body.

Burial 2 was a small child with a string of glass beads and a badly eroded fragment of worked shell on the chest.

Burial 3 was a tiny infant with a fragment of eroded conch shell on the chest and a string of glass beads.

Burial 4 was a small infant with a large string of beads, one large and two small brass discs on the chest, a projectile point, and a shell-tempered jar with a flaring rim.

Burial 5 was an adolescent or gracile adult female and contained one opaque turquoise blue bead.

Burial 6 was a child burial, perhaps a six-year-old, accompanied by a string of shell and glass beads.

Burial 7 was a burial of unrecorded age with a string of beads, two brass disc gorgets, brass beads, a spatulate celt, three projectile points, a biconcave stone disc, and a shell-tempered pot with two strap handles and small fillet strips.

Burial 8 was a burial of unrecorded age with a string of glass beads.

Burial 9 was a burial of unrecorded age with a string of glass beads and a necklace of 20 beads and a triangular pendant of brass or copper.

Burial 10 was a burial of unrecorded age accompanied by two flared-rim, incised pots and a string of glass beads.

Burial 11 was a burial of unrecorded age accompanied by two shell-tempered jars, one with folded and pinched rim, the other with notched lugs, and by a small brass disc gorget, a half of a brass gorget with a perforation near the edge for use as a pendant, and 89 glass beads.

Table A.1. Glass, shell, and brass beads from the Terrapin Creek site

Description	Kidd no.	Burial number											
		1	2	3	4	5	6	7	8	9	10	11	13
Turquoise blue	IIa40	61	33	7	63	1	18	5	33[a]	11	13	14	20
Transparent medium blue	IIa44	12	3	8	43		6	15		4	39	53	
Translucent navy blue	IIa55	3		2	9					1	5	8	
Transparent green	IIa28	1		2	2						1	1	
Opaque white	IIa13			5	1						1		
Transparent wine	IIa-				2						1	4	
Transparent amber	IIa-				3								
Opaque black	IIa6				1								
Colorless with white stripe	IIb18	2			3			2		1	3	1	
Translucent blue with 4 red and 4 white alternating stripes	IIb-						2						
Translucent blue with 3 red and 3 white alternating stripes	IIb-	1		1			2					1	
Transparent blue with 8–10 white stripes	IIb-				2							2	
Transparent blue with 5 white stripes	IIb-				5								
Transparent blue, spiral white stripe	IIb'-								1				
White with blue eyes	IIg4	2	1										
Turquoise with red and white eyes	IIg-	3	2					1				1	1

Description	Type												
Navy, 3 sets of white-red-white stripes	IIbb27											2	2
Gunmetal blue with 3 or 4 sets of white-red-white stripes	IIbb-			1									1
Small Nueva Cadiz Plain	IIIc-			1									
Faceted blue 7-layer chevron	IIIm-												1
Blue/white/blue	IVa16				1								
Transparent amber/blue	IVa-				1								
Transparent purple/blue	IVa-				1								
Blue/white/blue, 3 white stripes	IVb29				1								
Blue/white/blue, 2 red and 2 white alternating stripes	IVb-				1								
Blue/white/blue, 3 double red stripes alternating with 3 double white stripes	IVb-						1						
Blue/white/blue with eyes	IVg1		1										
Green 5-layer tumbled chevron	IVk6				3			2					
Total glass beads		85	42	27	144	1	29	25	35	18	62	89	21
Shell beads			30	7	178+		+	+		20			
Brass beads					1						20		

a. Sum of turquoise blue and transparent medium blue.

Burial 12 was an adult accompanied by two pottery vessels, two brass disc gorgets, and approximately 12 glass beads (unrecorded).

Burial 13 was a child accompanied by a stack of sherds, two brass discs, five or six brass conical bangles, and a string of 21 glass beads.

Burial 14 was a burial of unrecorded age accompanied by two pottery vessels and no European goods.

Burial 15 was a burial reportedly found by another collector which contained a piece of "copper." It is not known if there were additional artifacts, and I did not see the copper.

Burial 16 was a child aged 2–3 accompanied by seven brass discs and approximately three brass beads.

Burial 17 was accompanied by one brass gorget, 28 projectile points, and an incised jar, which, according to the notes, was classified Lamar Bold Incised but may have been shell tempered (I did not see it).

It should be noted that burials 1–5 and 7–11 were said to have been excavated from the same house. The impression given by the collectors was that the burials accompanied by European grave goods were only a small minority of the burials excavated and that they were clustered in a relatively small area. This fact could be interpreted to indicate a small historic component to the site, or it could mean that European goods were hoarded by a small segment of the community.

Bradford Ferry Site (1Ce73)

The Bradford Ferry Site was investigated as a part of the University of Alabama's Weiss Reservoir project (DeJarnette et al. 1973). During the winters of 1974–76, the water level of Lake Weiss was lowered, exposing numerous burials being disturbed by wave action. I recorded 29 burials recovered during this period by collectors from Alabama and Georgia. Many were in clusters, perhaps representing household units. It was not determined if they were buried in houses. Some of the burials had been vandalized. A summary of the glass beads found is contained in table A.2.

Burial 1 was an adult over age thirty (dental estimate). Near his knees was a brass gorget two inches in diameter with a large central perforation. Scattered in the pit were several glass beads.

Burial 2 was an adult accompanied by a thick iron chisel, 5 inches long, near the front of the skull. A cache of nine projectile points and a piece of red ocher were located near the legs. This burial may have contained two individuals, but poor bone preservation made confirmation impossible.

Burial 3 contained no preserved human remains, but the small pit size indicated the burial of a child. The pit contained a plain vessel with strap handle, a circular brass gorget 5.75 inches in diameter, and several glass beads.

Burial 4 was a child accompanied by a necklace of glass beads.

Burial 5 was an adult burial represented by teeth only. The burial was accompanied by a poorly preserved necklace of brass beads and a brass gorget. This burial was parallel to Burial 4.

Burial 6 was also poorly perserved but contained a rolled brass bracelet and three brass beads scattered in the pit.

Burial 7 was apparently a poorly preserved adult accompanied by a circular brass gorget 4.75 inches in diameter with a central perforation ⅜ inches in diameter.

Burial 8 was located approximately four feet north of Burial 7. In the south end of the pit was a string of glass beads. A few brass fragments were found near the beads.

Burial 9 was a child with no grave goods. The burial was oriented slightly east of north with head to the north.

Burial 10 contained only a few bone fragments, but the large pit size suggests an adult. Two pottery vessels were recovered: one was a jar with an "Easter basket" handle and the other a bold incised bowl with a smooth, snakelike rim effigy facing across the bowl to a square, luglike tail. This burial pit was oriented north-south with head probably to the north.

Burial 11 was a previously disturbed burial oriented north-south approximately two feet north of Burial 10. Three projectile points were found on the eastern undisturbed edge of the pit.

Burial 12 was located due south of Burial 10 and also oriented north-south. Burial 12 was accompanied by seven copper bangles, two Clarksdale bells (identified by Ian Brown), and a long string of necklace beads (not analyzed) that contained eye beads, blue beads, and gooseberry beads. At the southern end of the pit, a single-layer mass of seed beads was discovered, suggesting a beaded item had been placed in the grave. Beads were blue (some faceted) and "white" (colorless/white/colorless).

Burial 13 was due east of Burial 10. Grave goods include a brass gorget seven inches in diameter, two grit-tempered vessels, copper armbands, and 15 blue glass beads.

Table A.2. Glass beads from the Bradford Ferry site

Description	Kidd no.	Misc.[a]	Burial number									
			1	3	4	8	15	16	18	21	23	27
Opaque white	IIa13							1				
Opaque pale green	IIa-			2								
Transparent green	IIa28				P	2		2				
Turquoise blue	IIa40	P	1	7	P	P	13	11		58	14	1
Transparent blue	IIa44	P	1	2	P	P	9	32		5	5	1
Transparent navy blue	IIa55	P		2		P		2			1	1
Opaque white, metallic lustre	IIa-			1								
Translucent amber	IIa-	P										
Colorless with white stripes	IIb18	P						1				
Translucent green with 7 white stripes	IIb53		1									
Turquoise blue with 4 white stripes	IIb57									1		
Translucent blue with 2 red and 2 white alternating stripes	IIb71	P		3		2					4	
Translucent blue, 8–10 white stripes	IIb-	P	1				3	1				1
Translucent blue with 5 white stripes	IIb-						3			1		
Translucent blue with 3 red and 3 white alternating stripes	IIb-	P					3					
Fluted green melon with 3 white stripes	—						1					
White with blue eyes	IIg4							1				
Turquoise blue, red and white eyes	IIg-		1			1						
Green/white/colorless	IVa15					2						

Description	Type					(a)
Blue/colorless	IVa18					P
Blue/white /colorless (seed)	IVa-					P
Amber/white/blue, 3 sets of white-red-white stripes	IVbb-				1	1
Colorless/red/green	IVa5			5		
Red seed	IIa-	1				
Purple seed	IIa-		1			P
Translucent root beer, 4 white stripes	IIb-					1
Colorless, white stripes (olive)	IIb19					P
White, 3 sets of triple wavy blue stripes	IIb'-					1
Colorless/white/colorless (seed)	IVa11		1			P
Blue/white/blue	IVa16					P
Translucent purple/translucent blue	IVa-					P
Blue/white/blue with 8 eroded stripes	IVb-					1
Tumbled green 5-layer chevron	IVk6					P
Black seed	IIa		3			
Blue, pressed facets (pony size)	—	1				P
Colorless, pressed facets (pony)	—		1			P
Green, pressed facets (pony)	—					P
Purple, pressed facets (pony)	—					P
Navy blue seed	IIa-		122			P
Medium blue seed	IIa-		20			P

KEY: P = present (not quantified).

a. Miscellaneous burials and surface.

Burial 14 was a very small pit located approximately halfway between the University of Alabama trench and the eastern end of the site. A small string of beads was recovered, which included several transparent blue beads with red and white stripes.

Burial 15 was a child-size pit located when a large circular brass gorget was found on the surface. A string of glass beads accompanied the burial.

Burial 16 was a child burial (identified by pit size) located approximately 20 feet southeast of the cluster of burials 10–13. The pit was oriented northwest-southeast. The burial contained a string of glass beads. A conical brass bangle, possibly eroded out from this burial, was located some 8 inches to the north of the pit.

Burial 17 was a large pit located in the middle of the site south of the University of Alabama trench. A flexed adult, head to the east facing south, was wearing two large sheet brass armbands above the elbows. Further investigation revealed a second individual parallel to the first. A pottery vessel was located at the northeast corner of the pit along with teeth, skull fragments, and one glass bead. Another set of teeth was located in the north-central area of the pit, and a trade bead was found south of them. Another tooth, five glass beads, and a unifacial scraper were located near the northwestern corner of the pit. Thus Burial 17 apparently contained four individuals.

Burial 18 was located approximately 30 feet northeast of Burial 17. The pit was oriented east-west and contained a ceramic vessel in the eastern end. Just west of the vessel were numerous glass seed beads, and just west of the beads a small, circular brass gorget was located. Finally, a brass conical bangle was located in the northwestern corner of the pit. No bones were preserved, but the arrangements of artifacts and small pit size suggest an infant or child burial with head to the east.

Burial 19 was located approximately 10 feet east of Burial 18. The few bones recovered suggest an extended child burial with head to the south. At the southern end of the pit, an oval vessel with nodes and loop handles was recovered.

Burial 20 was oriented east-west and was just east of Burial 18. Bone preservation was extremely poor. A flaring-rim jar was located in the south-central area of the pit.

Burial 21 was an infant (determined by small pit size) placed just north of Burial 18 and parallel to it. Teeth were found in the south-central area. This burial was accompanied by numerous glass beads.

Burial 22 was due north and parallel to Burial 20 and due east of

Burial 21. The pit was oriented east-west, and the western end had been previously disturbed. The burial was placed head to the east. Fourteen projectile points, flint chunks, and flint flakes were found scattered in the pit. A large unifacial scraper and a conical stone pipe were found in the northeastern corner and a large limestone discoidal in the southeastern corner of the pit. The large pit size suggests that Burial 22 was an adult.

Burial 23 was located under water approximately 120 feet west of the University of Alabama trench. The pit fill was shoveled into a screen yielding 28 glass beads, teeth, and one projectile point. The teeth were identified by Clark Larsen as the remains of a three-year-old.

Burial 24 was a partially disturbed pit 57 inches by 23 inches. No human remains or grave goods were encountered, but the pit size and type of pit fill suggests a burial had been present.

Burial 25 was a small, disturbed pit 25 inches long located 37 inches northwest of Burial 24. Only one blue glass bead was recovered from this extremely shallow pit.

Burial 26 was located 41 inches to the northeast and parallel to Burial 25. The pit measured 40 inches by 20 inches. Bone preservation was very poor. No grave goods were located.

Burial 27 was located just east of the University of Alabama trench under water. It was approximately 10 yards north of Burial 15. The bottom of a pottery vessel, a projectile point, and one glass bead were seen under water. Shoveling into a screen located four additional beads. This burial had been almost completely destroyed by wave action.

Burial 28 was a burial located in a "storage pit." No artifacts appeared to be specific grave goods, but the collector reported numerous sherds in the pit fill.

Burial 29 was in a shallow pit 26 inches north-south and 20 inches east-west. The burial was flexed on the left side, head to the north. Four brass bangles were found around the head, and an iron celt was located near the face. A large quantity of red ocher and a large stone were located in the west-central area of the pit. Teeth from the burial were identified by Clark Larsen as the remains of a three-year-old.

Williams Island

Several sites on Williams Island, near Chattanooga, Tennessee, have been investigated for most of this century (see references in Smith

1976). Steve Hunter reported finding a burial with European and aboriginal grave goods in a village area. The burial was identified as a six-year-old child by Becky Laurens of Georgia State University. Grave goods included 12 conical brass bangles, 11 feet of shell beads (both conch and olivella), a small scallop shell, a variation of a Citico-style rattlesnake gorget (fig. 5.6), and the following glass beads: 10 turquoise blue, 17 transparent blue, 1 transparent green, 1 translucent dark blue with 4 red stripes, 1 translucent dark blue with 3 red stripes, and 2 eye beads (fully described in Smith 1982).

Appendix 2

Chronological Parameters of Lamar

Ceramics in the Wallace Reservoir

LATE prehistoric ceramics from the Wallace Reservoir area of the Oconee River drainage of the Georgia piedmont have been intensively studied by a number of authors (Smith 1978, 1981; Rudolph and Blanton 1980; Williams 1983). The Lamar period has been divided into three phases: Duvall, Dyar (with early and late subphases), and Bell (Smith 1978, 1981; Williams 1983). For the purpose of looking for change during the early historic period, only the Late Dyar (around 1525–1600) and Bell (1600–1670) phases need be considered here.

The Late Dyar phase is the sixteenth-century Lamar manifestation in the Wallace Reservoir area. The ceramic chronology for the Dyar phase is based on stratigraphic excavations into mound outwash and a house floor excavation at the Dyar site (Smith 1981). Ceramic types of the Dyar phase include Lamar Plain, Lamar Incised, Lamar Complicated Stamped, Coarse Plain, and Burnished Plain. The Early Dyar subphase also includes the type Morgan Incised. The Bell phase, defined at the Joe Bell site (Williams 1983), consists primarily of Lamar Incised and Plain ceramics.

Throughout the later portion of the Lamar period (Early Dyar, Late Dyar, Bell) several stylistic trends are in evidence in the ceramics. There was an overall reduction in the width of incised lines. Lamar Incised pottery in the Wallace Reservoir was subdivided into "bold incised" (line width greater than 2 mm), "medium incised" (1—2 mm), and "fine incised" (less than 1 mm). The Early Dyar subphase contained primarily bold incised ceramics with some medium incised. The Late Dyar phase had some percentage of all line categories, but fine incised was slightly more common than bold and medium incised made up some 70 percent of the incised pottery (Smith 1981:136). The frequency of fine incised pottery increased in the Bell phase at the expense of other types.

The type Morgan Incised (Smith 1981:189) occurred in the Duvall phase and the Early Dyar phase but was absent in the Late Dyar and Bell phases considered here. There was also a tendency for the number of incised lines to increase in Lamar Incised ceramics over time. Early Dyar phase vessels often had as few as two incised lines, while Bell phase vessels may have had more than twenty line elements.

Rim modes also tended to change through time. The early Lamar Duvall phase and Early Dyar phase vessels had folded rims decorated with hollow cane punctates, as well as folded and pinched rims. The folded and punctated rim mode disappeared by the Late Dyar phase, when rim folds with notching or scalloping were present. James Rudolph has demonstrated that the width of rim folds increased over time (Rudolph and Blanton 1980). During the Bell phase, a rim with a T-shaped flange, often incised on the upper surface, became popular and is an excellent marker for that phase.

There were also shifts in the frequency of complicated stamped decoration over time. Early Dyar phase levels at the Dyar site contain up to 20.5 percent stamped pottery, the Late Dyar phase less than 5 percent. Complicated stamped pottery is virtually unknown from Bell phase sites (Smith 1981; Williams 1983).

The trends are clear: less stamping, more and finer incised lines, and certain changes in rim decoration occurred over time. In addition, pipe smoking also increased dramatically in the Late Dyar and Bell phases; fine clay pipes are excellent markers of these phases.

The problem is how to determine the phase affiliation of a site based upon very small samples and preliminary laboratory analysis. All analyses were performed by trained laboratory personnel, but several individuals analyzed the sites so some subjective observations may not be consistent from site to site.

A set of rules was established to place sites into the appropriate components. Sites were assumed to be single component unless the ceramic counts strongly suggested otherwise. This decision undoubtedly masked some real situations, but for small sites with small collections it was the only reasonable choice.

Lamar sites believed to be single component were excluded as too early for this analysis (i.e., they belonged to the Duvall or Early Dyar phase) if they contained the type Morgan Incised, the folded and punctated rim mode, a predominance of bold over medium and fine incised, or a high frequency of complicated stamped ceramics.

Sites with a predominance of medium incised pottery, a small amount of complicated stamped sherds, and no folded and punctated rims were assigned to the Late Dyar phase.

Bell phase sites were distinguished by the presence of T-shaped rims, more fine incised than medium *or* bold incised, and virtually no complicated stamped sherds. Finally, sites having predominantly fine incised sherds but with complicated stamped sherds were assumed to be multicomponent.

After making phase identifications based on these criteria as applied to the preliminary analysis forms on file at the University of Georgia, James Rudolph graciously supplied additional rim analysis data. The inclusion of these data only changed the affiliation of a few sites, usually making them multicomponent. Thus the temporal analysis, although crude, appears to be successful and should be adequate for the broad purposes for which it is utilized here. Certainly a few individual sites may have been misidentified, but given the large sample size, such misidentifications are probably masked in the overall analysis.

References Cited

Adair, James
    1930   [1775] *The history of the American Indians.* New York: Promontory Press.
Baker, Steven G.
    1974   Cofitachique: fair province of Carolina: History and archaeology of the Carolina Indians. Master's thesis, University of South Carolina.
Bandera, Juan de la
    1569   Proceeding of the account which Captain Juan Pardo gave of the entrance which he made into the land of the Floridas. Archivo General de Índias 54-5-9. Copy in North Carolina State Archives, Raleigh. Translation by Paul Hoffman.
Battles, Mrs. Richard E.
    1969   One foot in a grave. *Journal of Alabama Archaeology* 15:35–38.
    1972   Copper and lithic artifacts. *Journal of Alabama Archaeology* 18:32–35.
Bennett, Charles, trans.
    1975   [1586] *Three voyages* by René Laudonnière (1586). Gainesville: University Presses of Florida.
Bennett, Monte
    1979   The Blowers site OND 1-4, an early historic Oneida settlement. *Bulletin, Chenango Chapter New York State Archaeological Association* 18(2):1–25.
Bourne, Edward Gaylord, ed.
    1922   *Narratives of the career of Hernando de Soto.* New York: Barnes.
Boyd, Mark F.
    1937   Expedition of Marcos Delgado, 1686. *Florida Historical Quarterly* 16:2–32.
Boyd, Mark F., Hale G. Smith, and John W. Griffin
    1951   *Here they once stood.* Gainesville: University of Florida Press.
Bradley, James W.
    1979   The Onondaga Iroquois, 1500–1655: A study in acculturative change and its consequences. Ph.D. diss., Syracuse University. Ann Arbor, Mich.: University Microfilms.
Brain, Jeffrey P.
    1975   Artifacts of the adelantado. *The Conference on Historic Site Archaeology Papers 1973* 8:129–38.
Brain, Jeffrey P., ed.
    1979   *Tunica treasure.* Papers of the Peabody Museum of American Archaeology and Ethnology 71. Cambridge: Harvard University Press.

165

Brain, Jeffrey P., Alan Toth, and Antonio Rodriguez-Buckingham
    1974   Ethnohistoric archaeology and the de Soto entrada into the Lower Missis-
            sippi Valley. *The Conference on Historic Site Archaeology Papers 1972* 7:232–89.
Brannon, Peter A., ed.
    1930   *Arrow points* 16(2).
    1935   *The southern Indian trade.* Montgomery, Ala.: Paragon Press.
Brehm, H. C.
    1981   *The history of the Duck River cache.* Tennessee Anthropological Society Miscel-
            laneous Paper 6. Knoxville, Tennessee.
Brown, Ian W.
    1979a   Historic artifacts and sociocultural change: Some warnings from the Lower
            Mississippi Valley. *The Conference on Historic Site Archaeology Papers 1978*
            13:109–21.
    1979b   Functional group changes and acculturation: A case study of the French
            and the Indian in the Lower Mississippi Valley. *Midcontinental Journal of Ar-
            chaeology* 4:147–65.
    1979c   Bells. In *Tunica treasure,* ed. Jeffrey P. Brain, 197–205, q.v.
Carmack, Robert, and John Weeks
    1981   The archaeology and ethnohistory of Utatlan: A conjunctive approach.
            American Antiquity 46:323–41.
Cook, Sherburne, and Woodrow Borah
    1960   *The Indian population of Central Mexico, 1531–1610.* Ibero-Americana 44.
            Berkeley: University of California Press.
Corkran, David
    1967   *The Creek frontier 1540–1783.* Norman: University of Oklahoma Press.
Cornett, B. Kenneth
    1976   Excavations at Tallassee (40Bt8): An historic Cherokee village site in East
            Tennessee. *Tennessee Archaeologist* 32:11–19.
Crane, Verner W.
    1981   *The southern frontier, 1670–1732.* New York: W. W. Norton.
Crosby, Alfred W., Jr.
    1972   *The Columbian exchange.* Westport, Conn.: Greenwood Press.
Curren, Cailup
    1982   The Alabama River phase: a review. In *Archaeology in Southwestern Alabama:
            A collection of papers,* ed. Cailup Curren, 103–14. Camden, Ala.: Alabama
            Tombigbee Regional Commission.
Curren, Cailup, Keith Little, and George Lankford
    1982   The route of the expedition of Hernando de Soto through Alabama. Re-
            vised draft of paper presented at the Southeastern Archaeological Confer-
            ence. Asheville, North Carolina, 1981.
Curren, Caleb
    1983   A theoretical model concerning the route of the expedition of Hernando de
            Soto through Alabama. Typescript in possession of the writer.
Deagan, Kathleen
    1972   Fig Springs: The mid-seventeenth century in North-Central Florida. *His-
            torical Archaeology* 6:23–46.
    1978   Archaeological strategy in the investigation of an unknown era: Sixteenth-
            century St. Augustine. Typescript, Florida State Museum, Gainesville.

Deetz, James
   1965   *The dynamics of stylistic change in Arikara ceramics.* Illinois Studies in Anthro-
          pology 4. Urbana: University of Illinois Press.
DeJarnette, David L.
   1975   *Archaeological salvage in the Walter F. George Basin of the Chattahoochee River in
          Alabama.* University, Ala.: University of Alabama Press.
DeJarnette, David L., and Asael T. Hansen
   1960   *The archaeology of the Childersburg site, Alabama.* Florida State University
          Notes in Anthropology 4. Tallahassee.
DeJarnette, David L., Edward Kurjack, and Bennie Keel
   1973   Archaeological investigations of the Weiss Reservoir of the Coosa River in
          Alabama. *Journal of Alabama Archaeology* 19:1–201.
Denevan, William M.
   1976   *The native American population of the Americas in 1492.* Madison: University of
          Wisconsin Press.
DePratter, Chester
   1983   Late prehistoric and early historic chiefdoms in the southeastern United
          States. Ph.D. diss., University of Georgia. Ann Arbor, Mich.: University
          Microfilms.
DePratter, Chester, and Marvin T. Smith
   1980   Sixteenth-century European trade in the southeastern United States: Evi-
          dence from the Juan Pardo expeditions (1566–1568). In *Spanish colonial
          frontier research,* ed. Henry F. Dobyns, 67–77. Albuquerque, New Mexico:
          Center for Anthropological Studies.
DePratter, Chester, Charles Hudson, and Marvin Smith
   1983   The route of Juan Pardo's explorations in the interior Southeast, 1566–
          1568. *Florida Historical Quarterly* 62:125–58.
   1985   The De Soto expedition: From Chiaha to Mabila. In *Alabama and the border-
          lands, from prehistory to statehood,* ed. Reid Badger and Lawrence Clayton,
          pp.108–27. Tuscaloosa: University of Alabama Press.
Dickens, Roy S.
   1979   *Archaeological investigations at Horseshoe Bend.* Special Publications of the Ala-
          bama Archaeological Society, no. 3.
Dobyns, Henry F.
   1963   An outline of Andean epidemic history to 1720. *Bulletin of the History of
          Medicine* 37:493–515.
   1966   Estimating aboriginal American population: An appraisal of techniques
          with a new hemispheric estimate. *Current Anthropology* 7:395–416.
   1983   *Their number become thinned.* Knoxville: University of Tennessee Press.
Evans, E. Raymond, Victor Hood, and Loretta Lautzenheiser
   1981   Preliminary excavations on the Audubon Acres site (40Ha84), Hamilton
          County, Tennessee. Typescript, Department of Anthropology, University of
          Tennessee, Chattanooga.
Fairbanks, Charles H.
   1952   Creek and Pre-Creek. In *Archeology of Eastern United States,* ed. James B.
          Griffin, 285–300. Chicago: University of Chicago Press.
   1958   Some problems of the origin of Creek Pottery. *Florida Anthropologist*
          11:53–63.
   1968   Early Spanish colonial beads. *The Conference on Historic Site Archaeology
          Papers 1967* 2:3–21.

Fenton, William N.
   1940   Problems arising from the historic northeast position of the Iroquois. *Smithsonian Miscellaneous Collections* 100:159–252.
Ferguson, Alice L. L.
   1940   An ossuary near Piscataway Creek. *American Antiquity* 6:4–13.
Fish, Suzanne, and Paul Fish
   1979   Historic demography and ethnographic analogy. *Early Georgia* 7:29–43.
Fitzgerald, William
   1982   A refinement of historic Neutral chronologies: Evidence from Shaver Hill, Christianson, and Dwyer. *Ontario Archaeology* 38:31–47.
Fleming, Victor K., and John A. Walthall
   1978   A summary of the historic aboriginal occupations of the Guntersville Basin, Alabama. *Southeastern Archaeological Conference Special Publication* 5:30–34.
Foster, George M.
   1960   *Culture and conquest.* Chicago: Quadrangle Books.
Fundaburk, Emma Lila
   1958   *Southeastern Indians life portraits.* Luverne, Ala.: E. L. Fundaburk.
Funkhouser, Gary
   1978   Paleodemography of the King site. Master's thesis, University of Georgia.
Gannon, Michael V.
   1965a   *The cross in the sand.* Gainesville: University Presses of Florida.
   1965b   Sebastian Montero, pioneer American missionary, 1566–1572. *The Catholic Historical Review* 51:335–53.
Geiger, Maynard
   1937   *The Franciscan conquest of Florida (1573–1618).* Washington, D.C.: Catholic University of America.
Goad, Sharon I.
   1978   Exchange networks in the prehistoric southeastern United States. Ph.D. diss., University of Georgia. Ann Arbor, Mich.: University Microfilms.
Goff, John H.
   1953   Some major Indian trading paths across the Georgia piedmont. *Georgia Mineral Newsletter* 6.
Goggin, John, and William Sturtevant
   1964   The Calusa: A stratified nonagricultural society. In *Explorations in Cultural Anthropology in Honor of George Peter Murdock,* ed. Ward Goodenough, 179–219. New York: McGraw-Hill.
Greer, E. S.
   1966   A Tukabahchee plate from the Coosa River. *Journal of Alabama Archaeology* 12:156–58.
Guthe, Alfred, and Marian Bristline
   1978   *Excavations at Tomotley, 1973–74, and the Tuskeegee Area: Two Reports.* University of Tennessee Department of Anthropology Report of Investigations, no. 24.
Hally, David J.
   1975   Archaeological investigation of the King site, Floyd County, Georgia. Report submitted to the National Endowment for the Humanities. Department of Anthropology, University of Georgia. Photocopy.
   1980   Archaeological investigation of the Little Egypt site (9Mu102), Murray County, Georgia, 1970–72 season. Submitted to the Heritage Conservation and Recreation Service, U.S. Department of the Interior.

1982 Archaeological investigations at the King site, Floyd County, Georgia. *National Geographic Society Research Reports* 14:303–9.

Hamilton, Henry, Jean Hamilton, and Eleanor Chapman
1974 *Spiro mound copper.* Missouri Archaeological Society Memoir 11. Columbia, Missouri.

Hamilton, T. M.
1980 *Colonial frontier guns.* Chadron, Nebraska: The Fur Press.

Hassan, Fekri A.
1981 *Demographic archaeology.* New York: Academic Press.

Hatch, James W.
1975 Social dimensions of Dallas burials. *Southeastern Archaeological Conference Bulletin* 18:132–38.
1976 The Citico site (40Ha65): A synthesis. *Tennessee Anthropologist* 1:75–103.

Hatch, James W., and Patrick Willey
1974 Stature and status in Dallas society. *Tennessee Archaeologist* 30:107–31.

Helms, Mary W.
1979 *Ancient Panama.* Austin: University of Texas Press.

Hemming, John
1978 *Red gold: The conquest of the Brazilian Indians, 1500–1760.* Cambridge, Mass.: Harvard University Press.

Hewitt, J. N. B.
1894 Era of the formation of the historic league of the Iroquois. *American Anthropologist* 7:61–67.

Hoffman, Bernard G.
1964 Observations on certain ancient tribes of the northern Appalachian province. *Bureau of American Ethnology Bulletin* 191:191–245.

Hoffman, Paul E.
1980 A new voyage of North American discovery: Pedro de Salazar's voyage to the Island of Giants. *Florida Historical Quarterly* 38:415–26.

Hosbach, Richard, and Stanford Gibson
1980 The Wilson site (OND9): A protohistoric Oneida Village. *Bulletin, Chenango Chapter New York State Archaeological Association* 18(4A).

Hudson, Charles M.
1976 *The southeastern Indians.* Knoxville: University of Tennessee Press.
1980 An unknown South: The world of sixteenth-century southeastern Indians. Paper presented at the Chancellor's Symposium, University of Mississippi.

Hudson, Charles M., M. T. Smith, and C. B. DePratter
1984 The route of the de Soto expedition from Apalachee to Chiaha. *Southeastern Archaeology* 3:65–77.

Hudson, C., M. Smith, D. Hally, R. Polhemus, and C. DePratter
1985 Coosa: A chiefdom in the sixteenth-century southeastern United States. *American Antiquity* 50: 723–37.

Humbard, Richard, and John Humbard
1965 Burial caches. *Journal of Alabama Archaeology* 11:133–42.

Hunt, George T.
1940 *The wars of the Iroquois: A study in intertribal trade.* Madison: University of Wisconsin Press.

Hunter, William A.
1978 History of the Ohio Valley. In *Northeast*, ed. Bruce G. Trigger, 588–93. Handbook of North American Indians, vol. 15, William G. Sturtevant, general editor. Washington, D.C.: Smithsonian Institution.

Jennings, Francis
    1978   Susquehannock. In *Northeast,* ed. Bruce G. Trigger, 362–67. Handbook of
            North American Indians, vol. 15, William G. Sturtevant, general editor.
            Washington, D.C.: Smithsonian Institution.
Jennings, Jesse D.
    1941   Chickasaw and earlier Indian cultures of Northeast Mississippi. *Journal of
            Mississippi History* 3:155–226.
Karklins, Karlis
    1974   Seventeenth-century Dutch beads. *Historical Archaeology* 8:64–82.
    1984   Glass beads from a late 16th–early 17th-century glasshouse in Amsterdam.
            Paper presented at the Society for Historical Archaeology, Williamsburg,
            Virginia.
Kenyon, Ian, and Thomas Kenyon
    1983   Comments on 17th-century glass trade beads from Ontario. In *Proceedings
            of the 1982 Glass Trade Bead Conference,* ed. Charles Hayes, 59–74. Rochester
            Museum Research Records, no. 16.
Kenyon, Walter A.
    1977   Some bones of contention: The Neutral Indian burial site at Grimsby. *Ro-
            tunda* 10(3):4–13.
    1982   *The Grimsby site.* Toronto: Royal Ontario Museum.
Kidd, Kenneth E.
    1954   Trade goods research techniques. *American Antiquity* 20:1–8.
Kidd, Kenneth, and Martha Kidd
    1970   *A classification system for glass beads for the use of field archaeologists.* In Cana-
            dian Historic Sites: Occasional Papers in Archaeology and History, no. 1,
            pp. 45–89.
Kneberg, Madeline
    1959   Engraved shell gorgets and their associations. *Tennessee Archaeologist*
            15:1–39.
Knight, Vernon J., and Sheree Adams
    1981   A voyage to the Mobile and Tomen in 1700 with notes on the interior of
            Alabama. *Journal of Alabama Archaeology* 27:32–56.
Knight, Vernon J., and Marvin T. Smith
    1980   Big Tallassee: A contribution to Upper Creek site archaeology. *Early Georgia*
            8:59–74.
Langford, James B., Jr., and Marvin T. Smith
    1986   Recent investigations in the core of the Coosa province. Paper presented at
            the Lamar Institute Conference on South Appalachian Mississippian,
            Macon, Georgia.
Lanning, John T.
    1935   *The Spanish missions of Georgia.* Chapel Hill: University of North Carolina
            Press.
Larson, Lewis H.
    1959   A Mississippian headdress from Etowah, Georgia. *American Antiquity*
            25:109–12.
    1971   Archaeological implications of social stratification at the Etowah site,
            Georgia. In *Approaches to the social dimensions of mortuary practices,* ed. James
            A. Brown, 58–67. Memoirs of the Society for American Archaeology,
            no. 25.

1972   Functional considerations of warfare in the Southeast during the Mississippi period. *American Antiquity* 37:383–92.

Ledbetter, Robert Jerald

N.d.   Wallace project backhoe testing program 1978. Department of Anthropology, University of Georgia. Typescript.

Lewis, Clifford, and Albert Loomie

1953   *The Spanish Jesuit mission in Virginia, 1570–1572.* Chapel Hill: University of North Carolina Press.

Lewis, T. M. N.

N.d.   The prehistory of the Chickamauga Basin. McClung Museum, University of Tennessee. Typescript.

1960   Editor's notes—Settico site on Little Tennessee River. *Tennessee Archaeologist* 16:93–103.

Lewis, T. M. N., and Madeline Kneberg

1941   *The prehistory of the Chickamauga Basin in Tennessee: A preview.* Tennessee Anthropological Papers 1. Knoxville: Division of Anthropology, University of Tennessee.

1946   *Hiwassee Island.* Knoxville: University of Tennessee Press.

Lindsey, Mrs. E. M.

1964   Cooper Farm salvage project. *Journal of Alabama Archaeology* 10:22–29.

Little, Keith, and Cailup B. Curren, Jr.

1981   Site 1Ce308: A protohistoric site on the Upper Coosa River in Alabama. *Journal of Alabama Archaeology* 27:117–24.

Lyon, Eugene

1976   *The enterprise of Florida.* Gainesville: University Presses of Florida.

1981   Spain's sixteenth-century North American settlement attempts: A neglected aspect. *Florida Historical Quarterly* 59:275–91.

Mason, Carol I.

1963   A reconsideration of Westo-Yuchi identification. *American Anthropologist* 65:1342–46.

Mathews, Davis S.

1984   The King site battle victims: The discovery of De Soto in Georgia. Paper presented at the annual meeting of the Southern Anthropological Society, Atlanta.

Milanich, Jerald T.

1978   The western Timucua: Patterns of acculturation and change. In *Tacachale,* ed. J. T. Milanich and Samuel Proctor, 59–88, q.v.

Milanich, Jerald T., and Samuel Proctor, eds.

1978   *Tacachale: Essays on the Indians of Florida and Southeastern Georgia during the historic period.* Gainesville: University Presses of Florida.

Milfort, Louis Le Clerk

1972   [1802] *Memoirs; or, a quick glance at my various travels and my sojourn in the Creek Nation.* Ed. and trans. Ben C. McCary [1959]. Savannah, Ga.: Beehive Press.

Milner, George G.

1980   Epidemic disease in the postcontact Southeast: A reappraisal. *Midcontinental Journal of Archaeology* 5:39–56.

Moore, Clarence B.

1900   Certain aboriginal remains of the Alabama River. *Journal of the Academy of Natural Sciences of Philadelphia,* 2d ser. 9(3).

1915   Aboriginal sites on Tennessee River. *Journal of the Academy of Natural Sciences of Philadelphia* 16:169–427.

Moorehead, Warren K.

1932   *Etowah papers.* New Haven, Conn.: Department of Archaeology, Phillips Academy.

Morrell, L. Ross

1964   Two historic island sites in the Coosa River. *Florida Anthropologist* 17:75–76.

1965   *The Woods Island site in southeastern acculturation, 1625–1800.* Florida State University Notes in Anthropology, no. 11.

Muller, Jon D.

1966   Archaeological analysis of art styles. *Tennessee Archaeologist* 22:25–39.

Myer, William C.

1928   *Indian trails of the Southeast.* Bureau of American Ethnology Annual Report no. 42. Washington, D.C.

Naroll, Raoul

1962   Floor area and settlement populations. *American Antiquity* 27:587–89.

Peebles, Christopher, and Susan M. Kus

1977   Some archaeological correlates of ranked societies. *American Antiquity* 42:421–48.

Perdue, Theda

1979   *Slavery and the evolution of Cherokee society 1540–1866.* Knoxville: University of Tennessee Press.

Phillips, Philip, James A. Ford, and James B. Griffin

1951   *Archaeological survey in the Lower Mississippi alluvial valley, 1940–1947.* Papers of the Peabody Museum of American Archaeology and Ethnology 25. Cambridge, Mass.: Harvard University Press.

Polhemus, Richard

1982   The early historic period in the East Tennessee Valley. Typescript in possession of the writer.

Pratt, Peter P.

1961   *Oneida Iroquois glass trade bead sequence, 1585–1745.* Rome, New York: Fort Stanwix Museum.

1976   *Archaeology of the Oneida Iroquois,* I. Occasional Publications in Northeastern Anthropology, no. 1. George's Mills, New Hampshire: Man in the Northeast, Inc.

Priestley, Herbert I.

1928   *The Luna papers: Documents relating to the expedition of Don Tristan de Luna y Arellano for the conquest of La Florida in 1559–1561.* 2 vols. Florida State Historical Society Publication no. 8. DeLand, Florida.

Quimby, George I., and Alexander Spoehr

1951   Acculturation and material culture. *Fieldiana: Anthropology* 36:107–47.

Ramenofsky, Ann F.

1982   The archaeology of population collapse: Native American response to the introduction of infectious disease. Ph.D. diss., University of Washington. Ann Arbor, Mich.: University Microfilms.

Rice, Orleans L.

1977   Trade goods with a Dallas Phase burial: Salvage archaeology at 40Mr12. *Tennessee Archaeologist* 33:17–22.

Rudolph, James, and Dennis Blanton
1980   A discussion of Mississippian settlement in the Georgia piedmont. *Early Georgia* 8:14–36.

Salo, Lawr V.
1969   Archaeological investigations in the Tellico Reservoir, Tennessee, 1967–1968: An interim report. Department of Anthropology, University of Tennessee.

Sauer, Carl Ortwin
1971   *Sixtenth-century North America*. Berkeley: University of California Press.
1980   *Seventeenth-century North America*. Berkeley: Turtle Island.

Scarry, C. Margaret
1983   Analysis of the floral remains from the 1982 Santa Elena (38Bu162) excavations. Appendix 2 in *Revealing Santa Elena 1982*, by Stanley South, 113–43. Research Manuscript Series 188. Institute of Archeology and Anthropology, University of South Carolina.

Schroedl, Gerald F., and Richard Polhemus
1977   A summary and preliminary interpretation of archaeological investigations at the Toqua site (40Mr6). Report Submitted to the National Park Service. University of Tennessee. Photocopy.

Seckinger, Ernest W.
1975   Preliminary report on the social dimensions of the King site mortuary practices. *Southeastern Archaeological Conference Bulletin* 18: 67–73.
1977   Social complexity during the Mississippian period in Northwest Georgia. Master's thesis, University of Georgia.

Service, Elman R.
1954   *Spanish-Guaraní relations in early colonial Paraguay*. Ann Arbor: University of Michigan Press.
1962   *Primitive social organization: An evolutionary perspective*. New York: Random House.

Shapiro, Gary N.
1983   Site variability in the Oconee province: A Late Mississippian society of the Georgia piedmont. Ph.D. diss., University of Florida. Ann Arbor, Mich.: University Microfilms.

Sheldon, Craig T., Jr.
1974   The Mississippian-historic transition in central Alabama. Ph.D. diss., University of Oregon. Ann Arbor, Mich.: University Microfilms.

Sheldon, Elisabeth
1978   Childersburg: Evidence of European contact demonstrated by archaeological plant remains. *Southeastern Archaeological Conference Special Publication* 5:28–29.

Siegel, Charles
N.d.   Producing a sampling scheme for the Wallace project subsurface survey. Department of Anthropology, University of Georgia. Typescript.

Smith, Buckingham
1968   *Narratives of De Soto*. Gainesville, Fla.: Palmetto Books.

Smith, Hale G.
1956   *The European and the Indian*. Florida Anthropological Society Publications, no. 4. Gainesville.

1973   Analysis of the Lamar site (9Bi7) materials at the Southeastern Archae-
           ological Center. Submitted to the National Park Service, Contract no.
           CX500031136, Tallahassee, Florida.

Smith, Marvin T.

1975   European materials from the King site. *Southeastern Archaeological Confer-
           ence Bulletin* 18:63–66.

1976   The route of De Soto through Tennessee, Georgia, and Alabama: The evi-
           dence from material culture. *Early Georgia* 4:27–48.

1977   The early historic period (1540–1670) on the Upper Coosa River drainage
           of Alabama and Georgia. *The Conference on Historic Site Archaeology Papers
           1976* 11:151–67.

1978   The development of Lamar ceramics in the Wallace Reservoir: The view
           from the Dyar site, 9Ge5. Paper presented at the 35th Southeastern Ar-
           chaeological Conference, Knoxville, Tennessee.

1979a   Glass trade beads from site 9Ge948, Wallace Reservoir, Georgia. MS, Labo-
           ratory of Archaeology. University of Georgia.

1979b   European artifacts from the Little Egypt site. In *Archaeological investigations
           of the Little Egypt site (9Mu102), Murray County, Georgia, 1970–1972 seasons,*
           ed. David J. Hally, 592–602. Report to the National Park Service. Depart-
           ment of Anthropology, University of Georgia.

1981   *Archaeological investigations at the Dyar site, 9Ge5.* Wallace Reservoir Project
           Contribution no. 11. Department of Anthropology, University of Georgia.

1982   "Eye" beads in the Southeast. *The Conference on Historic Site Archaeology
           Papers 1979* 14:116–27.

1983   Chronology from glass beads: The Spanish period in the Southeast, 1513–
           1670. In *Proceedings of the 1982 Glass Trade Bead Conference,* ed. Charles
           Hayes, 147–58. Rochester Museum Research Records, no. 16.

n.d.   European artifacts from the Plum Grove Site, 40Wg17. MS in possession of
           author.

Smith, Marvin T., and Mary Elizabeth Good

1982   *Early sixteenth-century glass beads in the Spanish colonial trade.* Greenwood,
           Miss.: Cottonlandia Museum.

Smith, Marvin T., and Steve A. Kowalewski

1980   Tentative identification of a prehistoric "province" in piedmont Georgia.
           Early Georgia 8:1–13.

South, Stanley

1980   *The discovery of Santa Elena.* Research Manuscript Series no. 165. Institute of
           Archeology and Anthropology, University of South Carolina.

Social Science Research Council (SSRC) Summer Seminar on Acculturation

1954   Acculturation: An exploratory formulation. *American Anthropologist* 56:
           973–1002.

Steele, W. S., and M. F. Hullender

1960   Gorgets from the Sylacauga water works site. *Journal of Alabama Archaeology*
           6:38–39.

Steponaitis, Vincas P.

1978   Location theory and complex chiefdoms: A Mississippian example. In *Mis-
           sissippian settlement patterns,* ed. Bruce D. Smith, 417–53. New York: Aca-
           demic Press.

Steward, Julian H.

1942   The direct historical approach to archaeology. *American Antiquity* 7:337–43.

1948   The circum-Caribbean tribes: an introduction. In *Handbook of North American Indians* 4, *The circum-Caribbean tribes*) ed. J. H. Steward, 1-41. Bureau of American Ethnology Bulletin 143. Washington, D.C.

Steward, Julian H., and Louis Faron
1959   *Native peoples of South America.* New York: McGraw-Hill.

Swanton, John R.
1922   *Early history of the Creek Indians and their neighbors.* Bureau of American Ethnology Bulletin 73. Washington, D.C.

1928   *Social organization and social usages of the Indians of the Creek Confederacy.* Bureau of American Ethnology Annual Report no. 42. Washington, D.C.

1939   *Final report of the United States De Soto Expedition Commission.* House Document 71, 76th Cong., 1st sess., Washington, D.C.

1946   *Indians of the Southeast.* Bureau of American Ethnology Bulletin 137. Washington, D.C.

Tally, Lucy
1975   Preliminary demographic analysis of the King site burial population. *Southeastern Archaeological Conference Bulletin* 18:74–75.

Tennessee Archaeological Society
1982   Village of Chiaha: An update. *Tennessee Archaeological Society Newsletter* 27(6):1.

Thomas, Alfred Barnaby
1982   *Alonso de Posada Report, 1686: A description of the area of the present southern United States in the late seventeenth century.* Pensacola, Fla.: Perdido Bay Press.

Thomas, Cyrus
1894   *Report on the mound exploration of the Bureau of American Ethnology.* Bureau of American Ethnology Annual Report no. 12. Washington, D.C.

Trigger, Bruce G.
1976   *The children of Aataentsic.* 2 vols. Montreal: McGill-Queens University Press.

1978   Early Iroquoian contacts with Europeans. In *Northeast,* ed. Bruce G. Trigger, 344–56. Handbook of North American Indians, vol. 15, William G. Sturtevant, general editor. Washington, D.C.: Smithsonian Institution.

Trimble, Stanley W.
1969   Culturally accelerated erosion on the Middle Georgia piedmont. Master's thesis, University of Georgia.

Varner, John G., and Jeannette Varner
1951   *The Florida of the Inca.* Austin: University of Texas Press.

Walthall, John A.
1981   *Galena and aboriginal trade in Eastern North America.* Illinois State Museum Scientific Papers 17. Springfield, Ill.

Wauchope, Robert
1956   *Seminars in archaeology: 1955.* Society for American Archaeology Memoir no. 11. Salt Lake City.

1966   *Archaeological survey of Northern Georgia.* Society for American Archaeology Memoir no. 21. Washington, D.C.

Webb, William S.
1938   *An archaeological survey of the Norris Basin in Eastern Tennessee.* Bureau of American Ethnology Bulletin 118. Washington, D.C.

Webb, William S., and Charles Wilder
1951   *An archaeological survey of Guntersville Basin on the Tennessee River in Northern Alabama.* Lexington: University of Kentucky Press.

Wenhold, Lucy L.
1936 A 17th-century letter of Gabriel Diaz Vara Calderon, Bishop of Cuba, describing the Indians and Indian missions of Florida. *Smithsonian Miscellaneous Collections* 95(16):1–14.

White, John R.
1975 Historic contact sites as laboratories for the study of culture change. *The Conference on Historic Site Archaeology Papers 1974* 9:153–63.

White, Marian E.
1978 Erie. In *Northeast,* ed. Bruce G. Trigger, 412–17. Handbook of North American Indians, vol. 15, William G. Sturtevant, general editor. Washington, D.C.: Smithsonian Institution.

Willey, Pat, Mark Guagliardo, and William Bass
1978 Brakebill mound, near Knoxville, Tennessee: A history of the mound and description of two recently recovered skeletons. *Tennessee Anthropologist* 3:145–67.

Williams, John Mark
1981 *Archaeological investigations at the Joe Bell site, 9Mg28.* Wallace Reservoir Contributions, no. 18. Department of Anthropology, University of Georgia.
1983 The Joe Bell site: Seventeenth-century lifeways on the Oconee River. Ph.D. diss., University of Georgia. Ann Arbor, Mich.: University Microfilms.
1984 *Archaeological excavations at Scull Shoals Mounds, Georgia.* Cultural Resources Report no. 6. U.S. Department of Agriculture, Forest Service Southern Region.

Williams, Samuel C.
1928 *Early travels in the Tennessee country, 1540–1800.* Johnson City, Tenn.: Watauga Press.

Wilson, Jack
1980 Excavations at Upper Saura Town, a Siouan village on the Dan River. Paper presented at the 37th Southeastern Archaeological Conference, New Orleans.

Wolf, Eric R.
1982 *Europe and the people without history.* Berkeley: University of California Press.

Woodward, Arthur
1932 The value of Indian trade goods in the study of archaeology. *The Pennsylvania Archaeologist* 3(1):8–9, 16–19.

Wray, Charles F.
1973 *Manual for Seneca Iroquois archaeology and slide set.* Rochester, New York: Cultures Primitive.

Wray, Charles F., and Harry L. Schoff
1953 A preliminary report on the Seneca sequence in western New York, 1550–1687. *Pennsylvania Archaeologist* 23:53–63.

Wright, J. Leitch, Jr.
1981 *The only land they knew.* New York: The Free Press.

Zahler, James W., Jr.
1976 A morphological analysis of a protohistoric-historic skeletal population from St. Simons Island, Georgia. Master's thesis, University of Florida.

Index